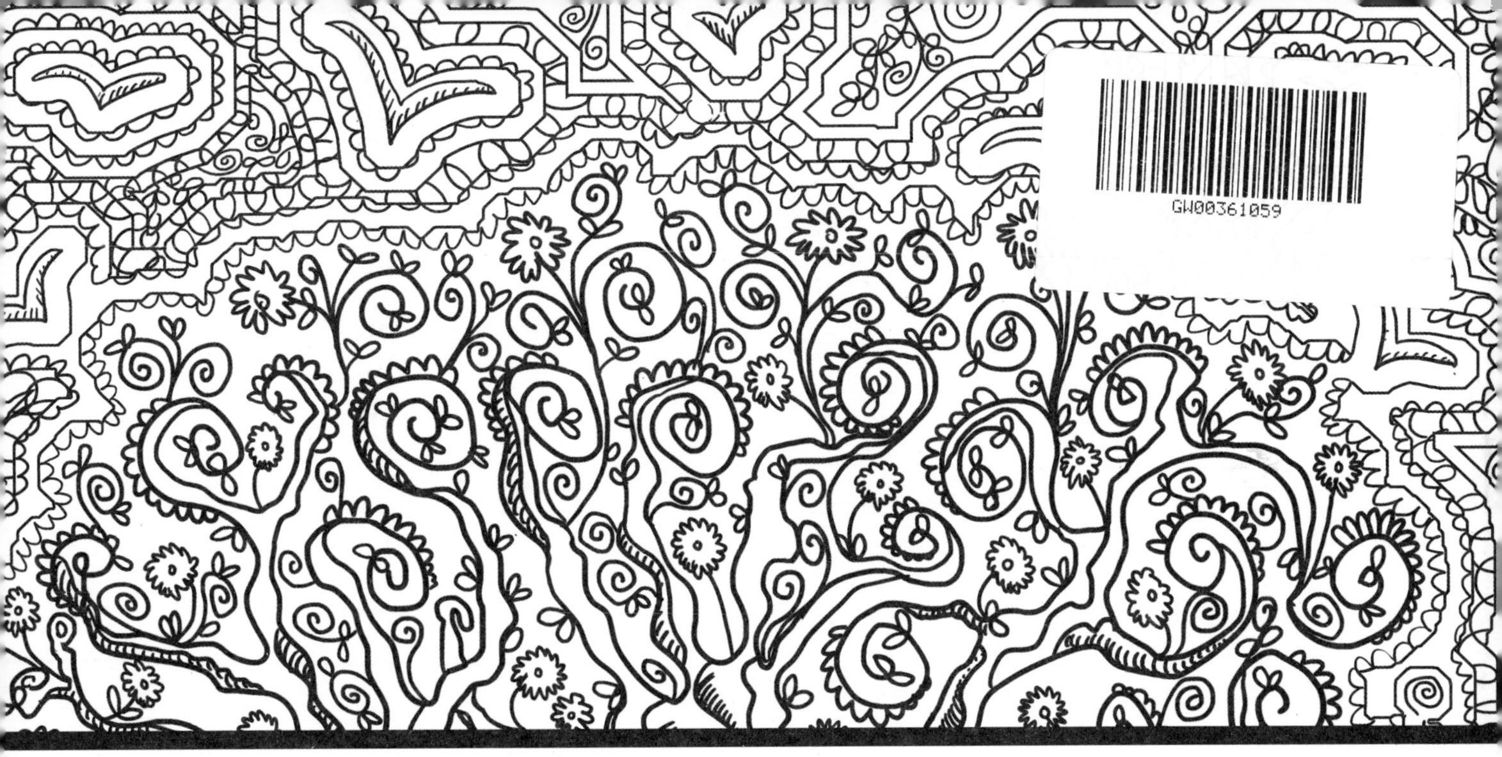

The art of COLOURING

Relax and create.

Illustrated by Jo Joof

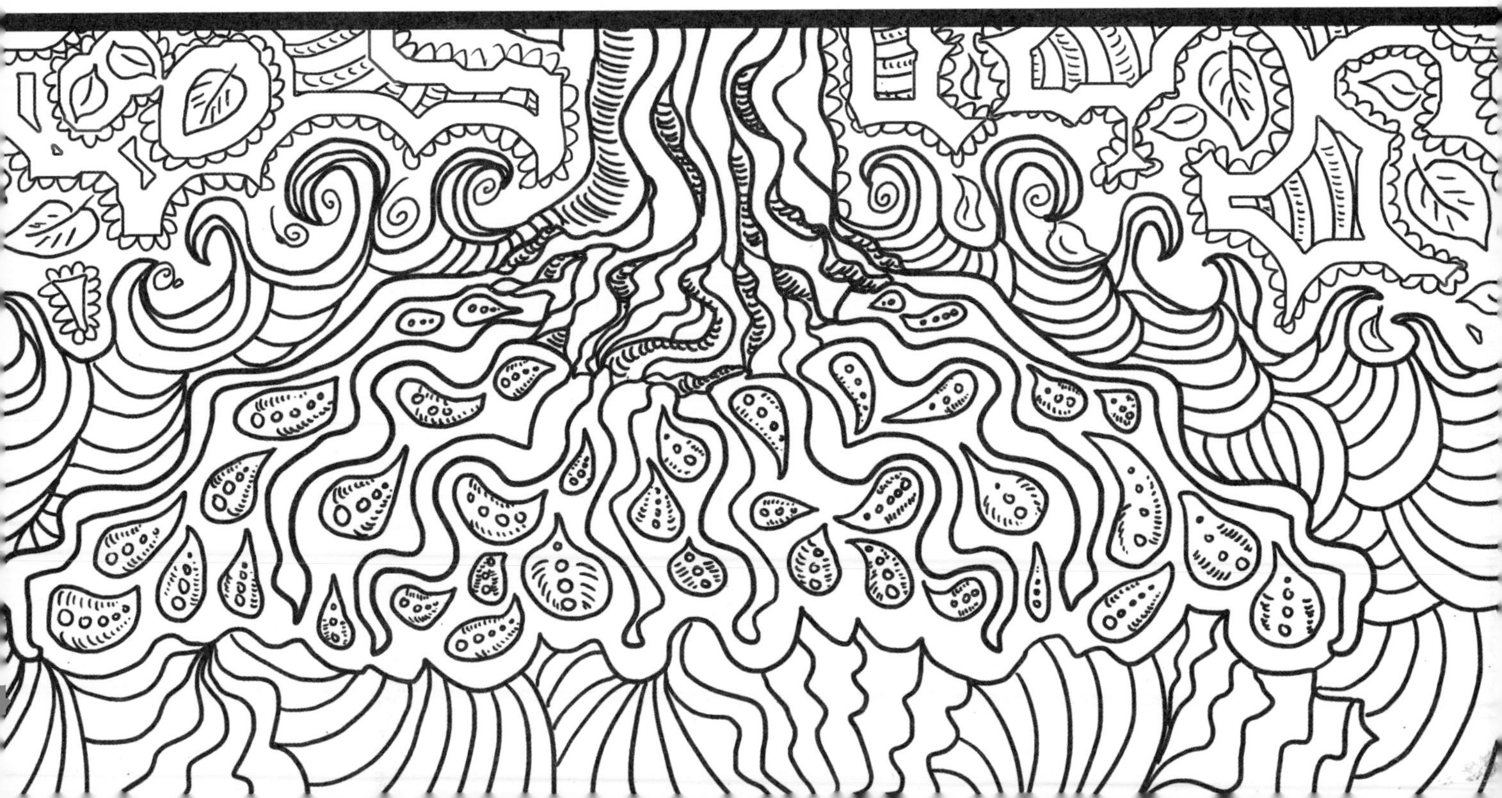

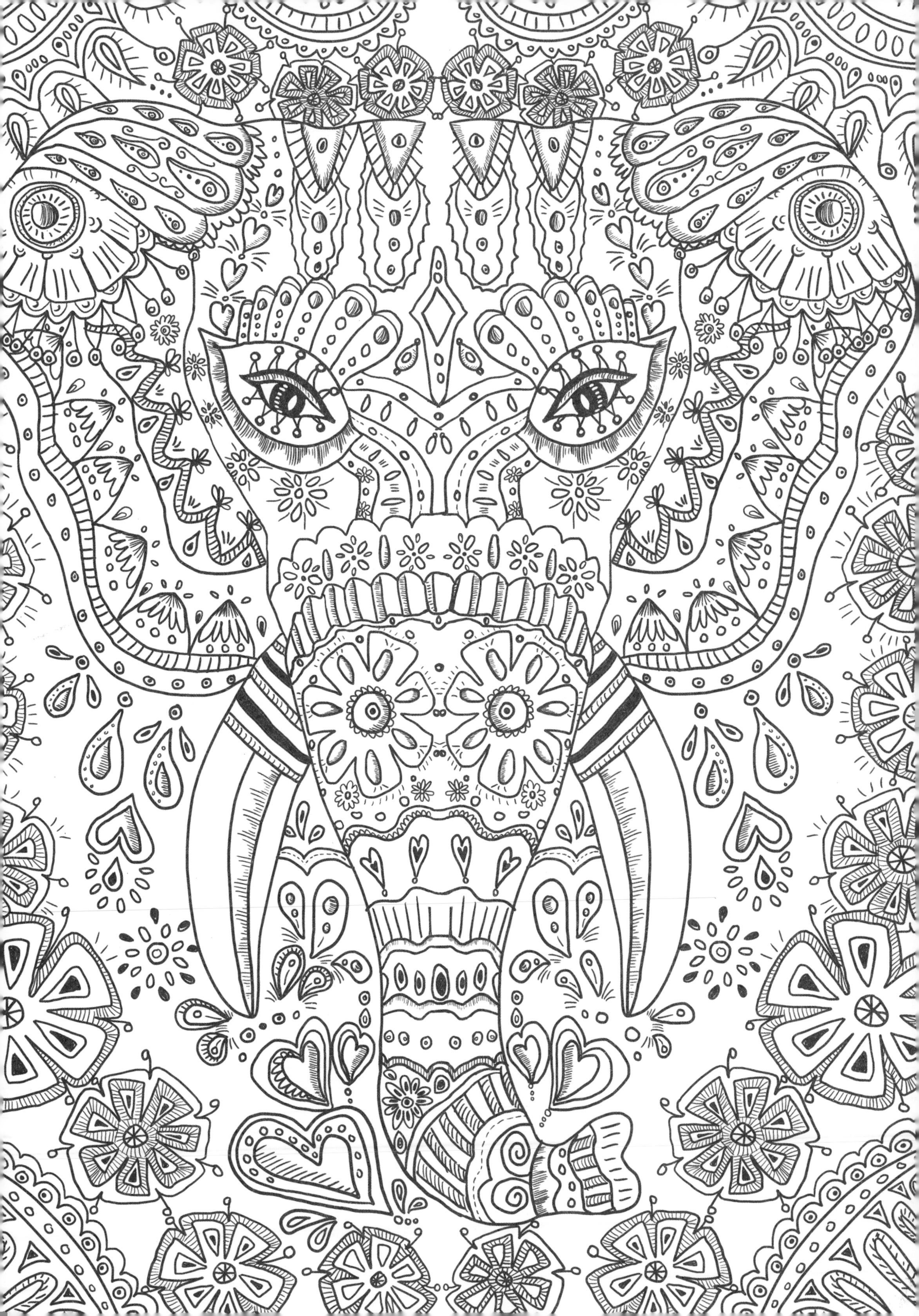

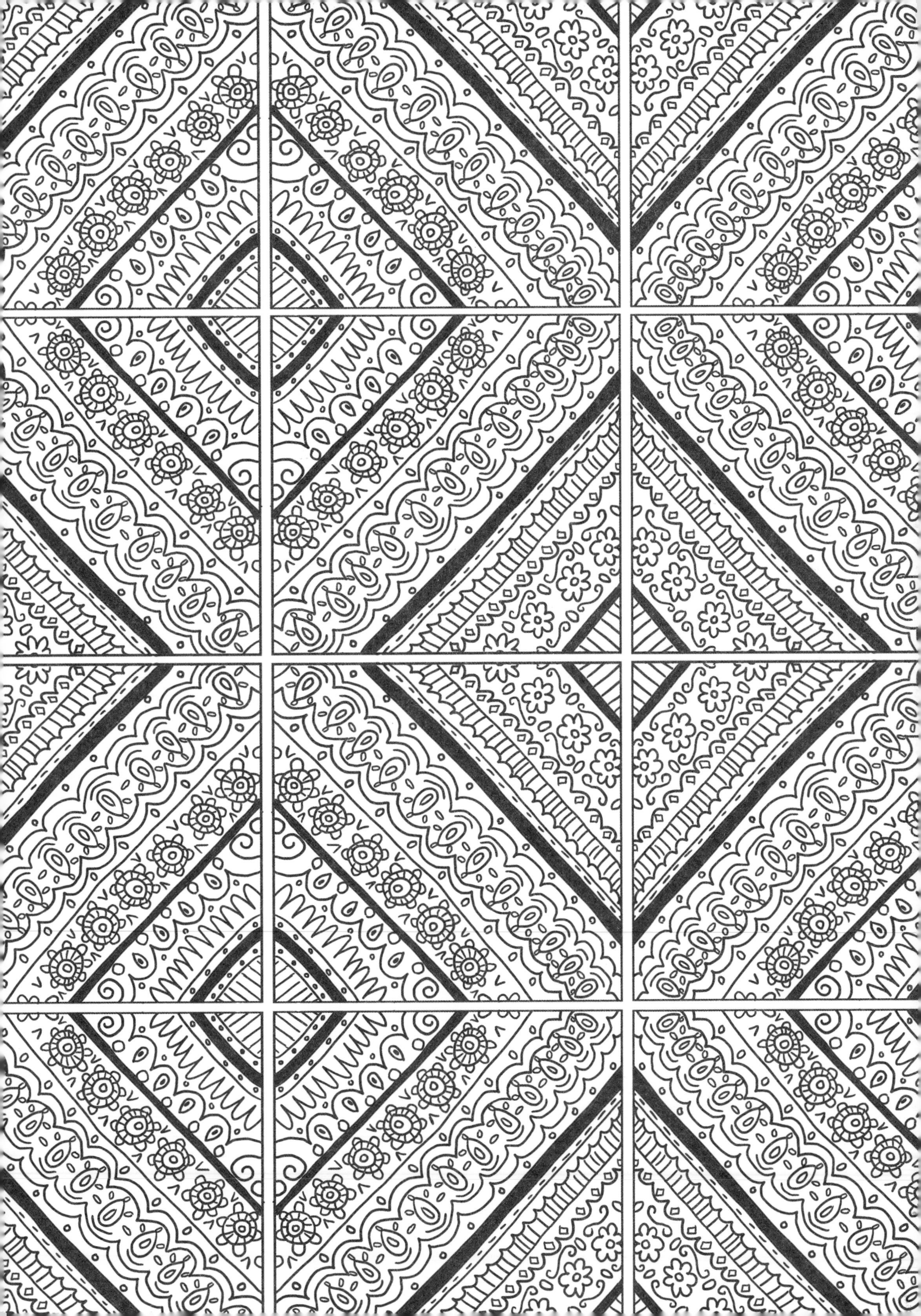

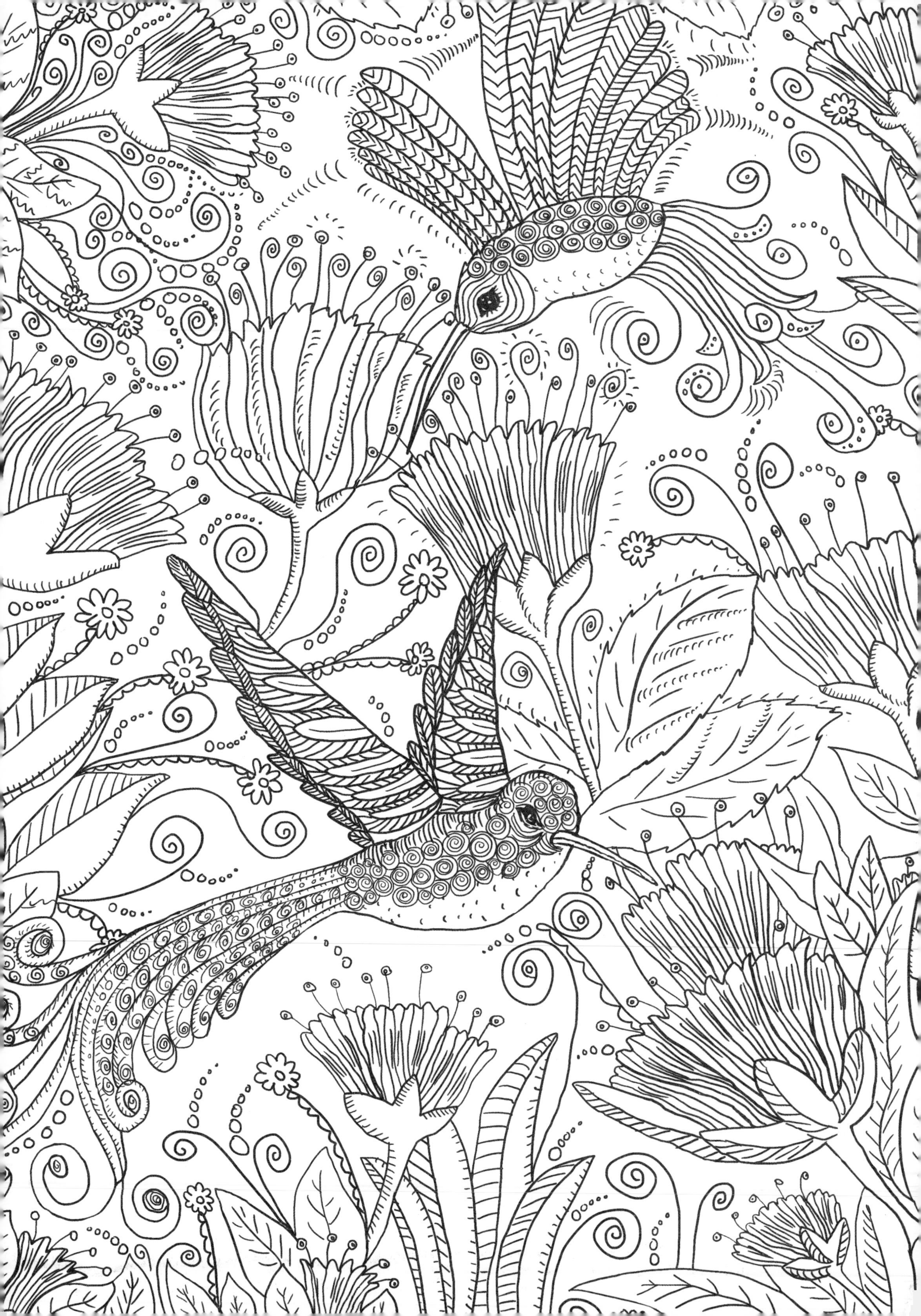

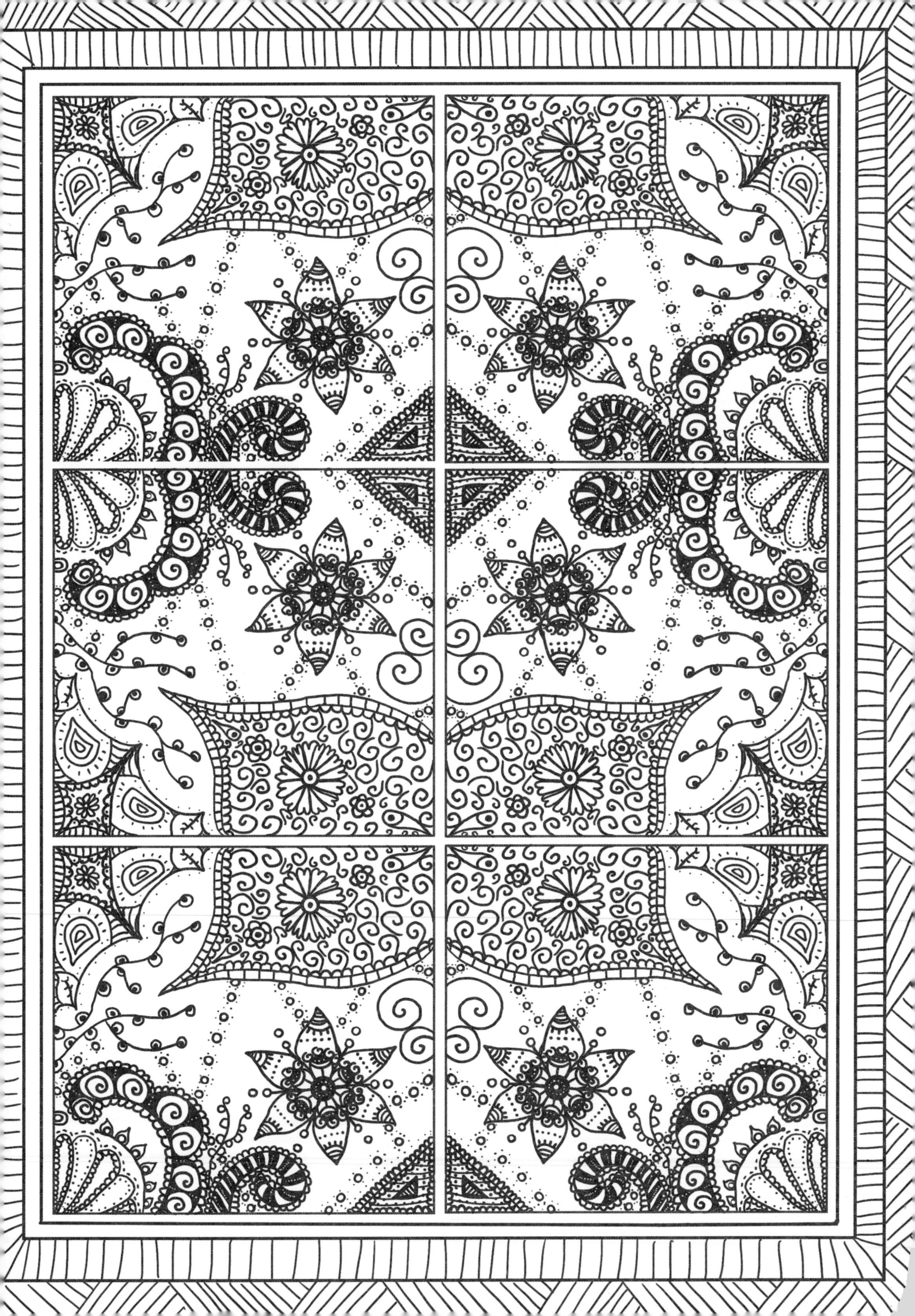

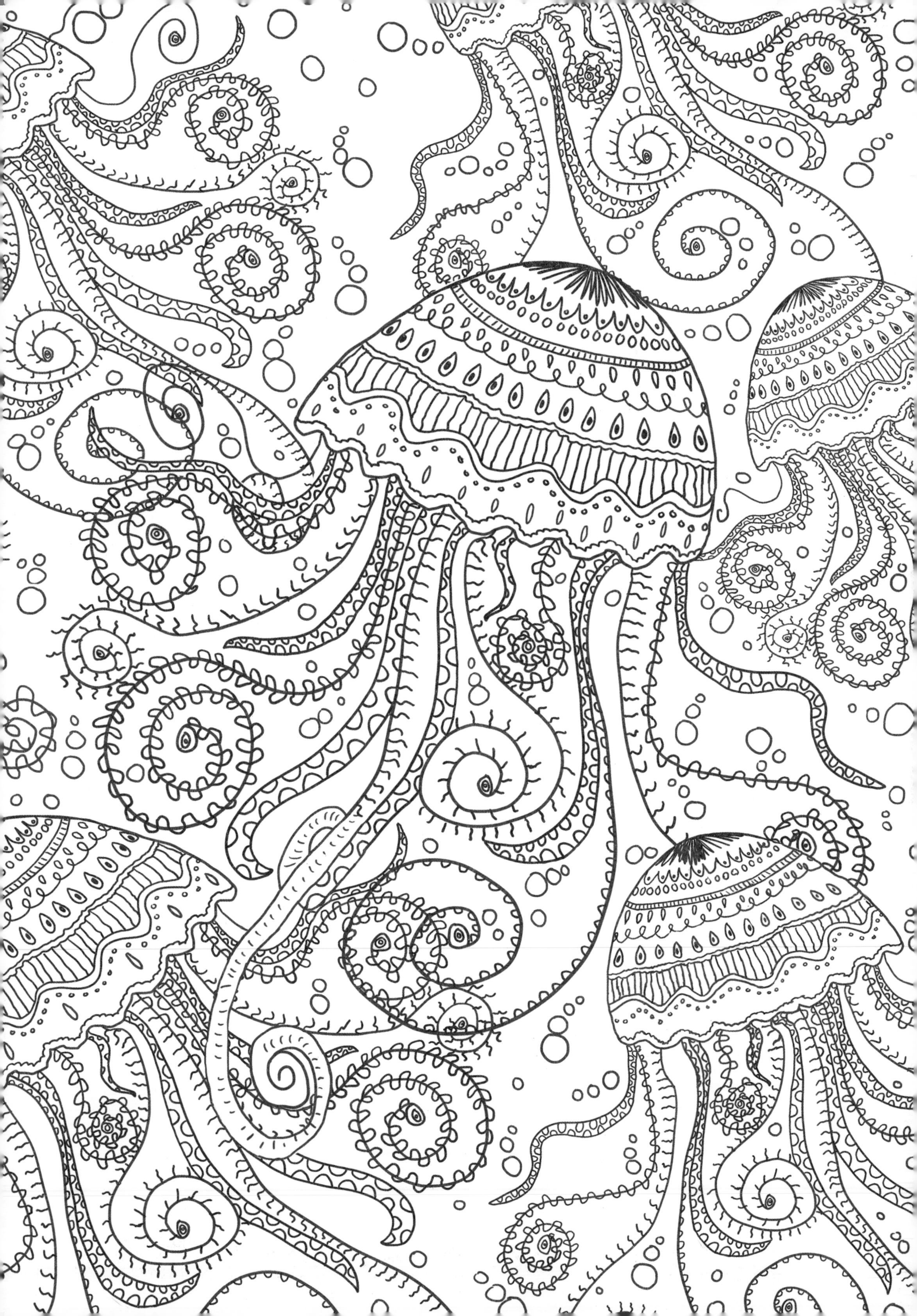

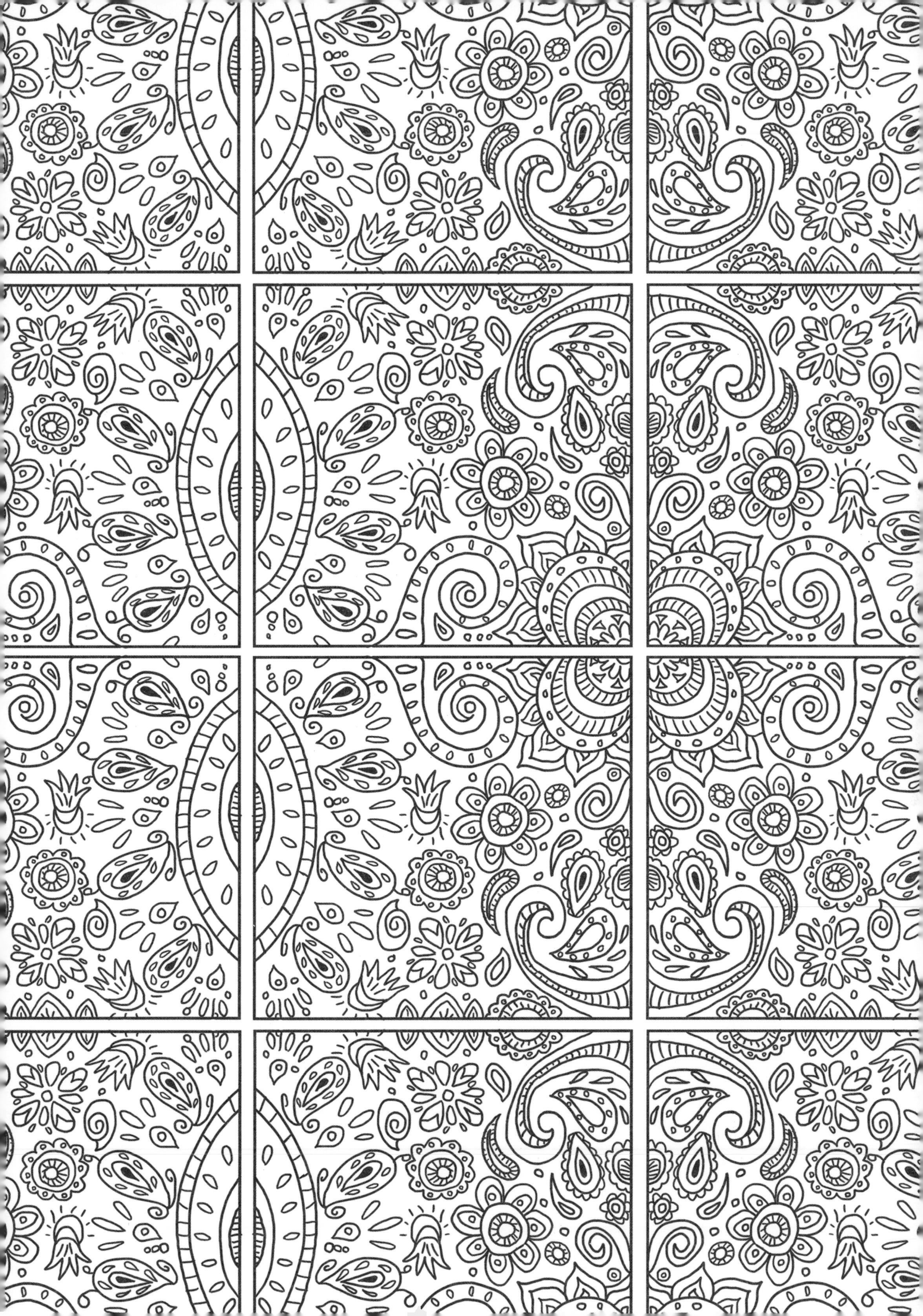

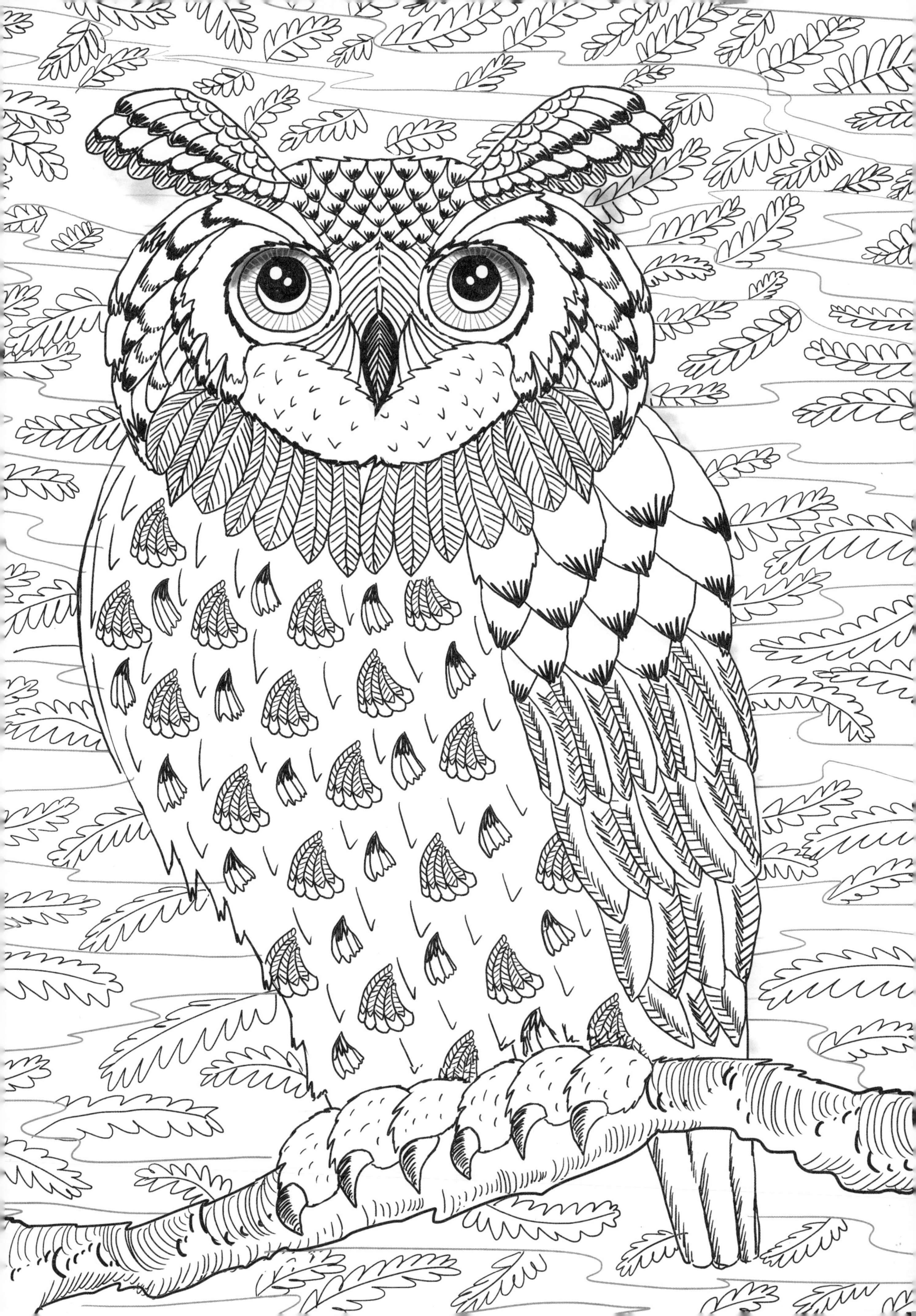

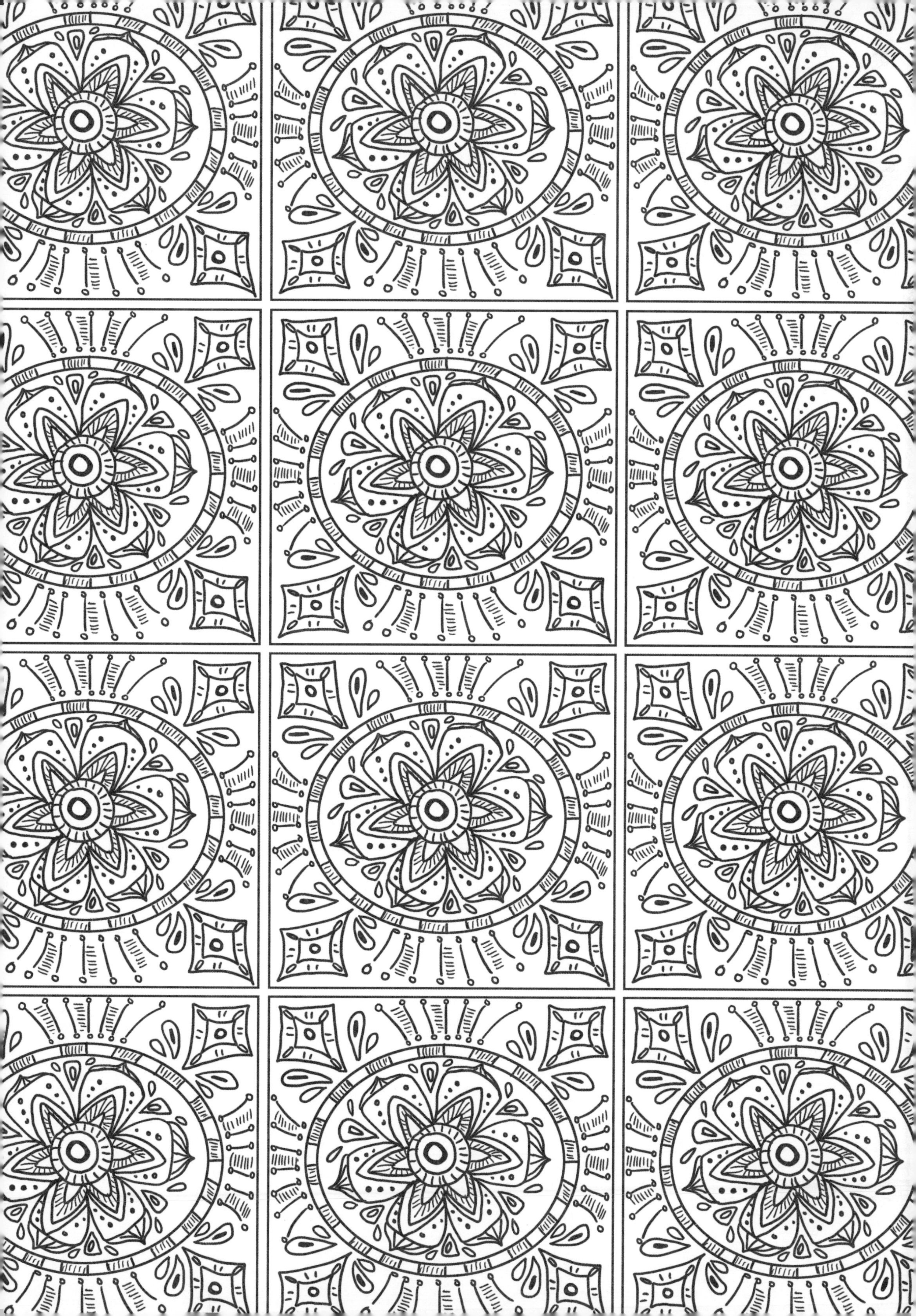

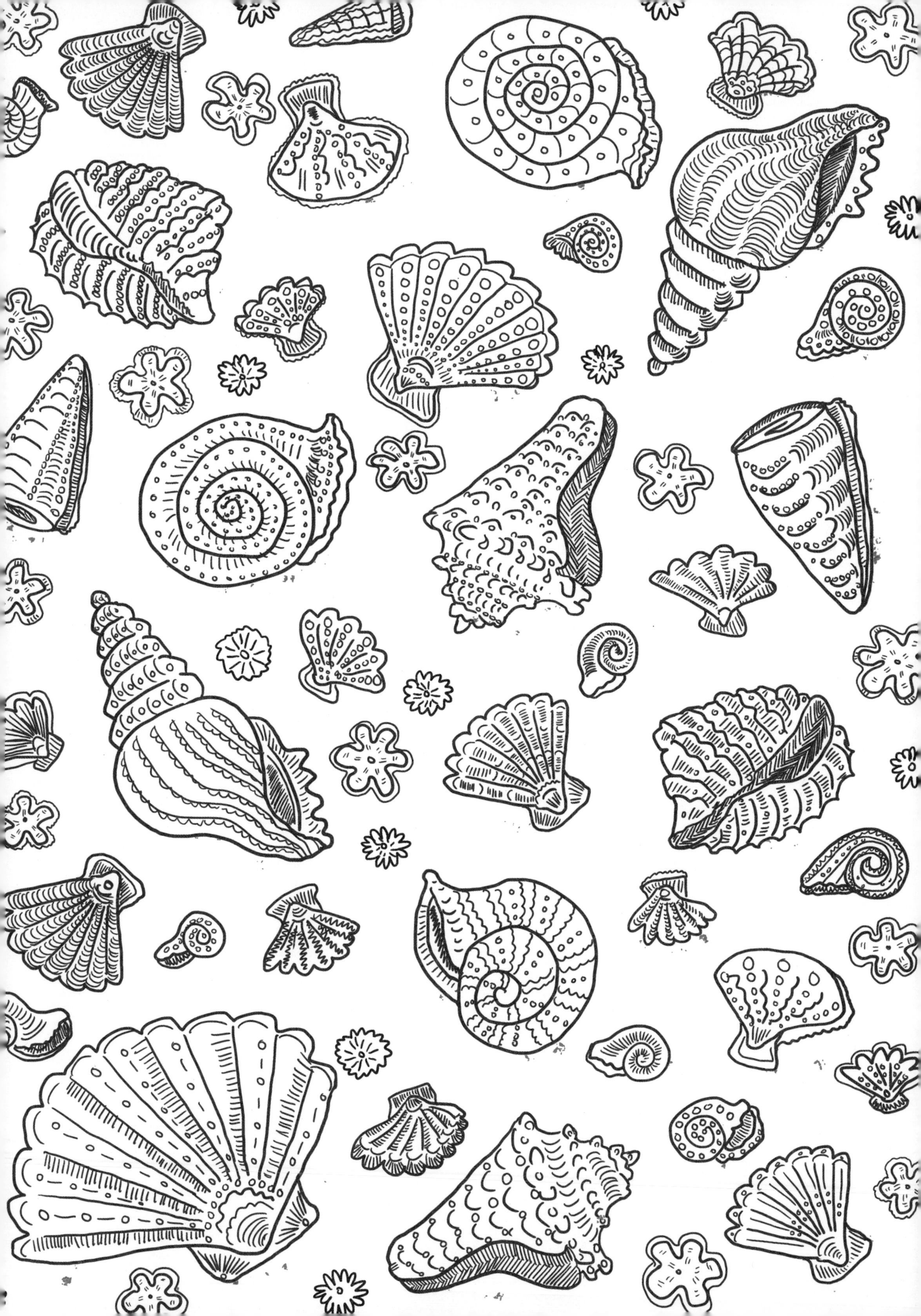

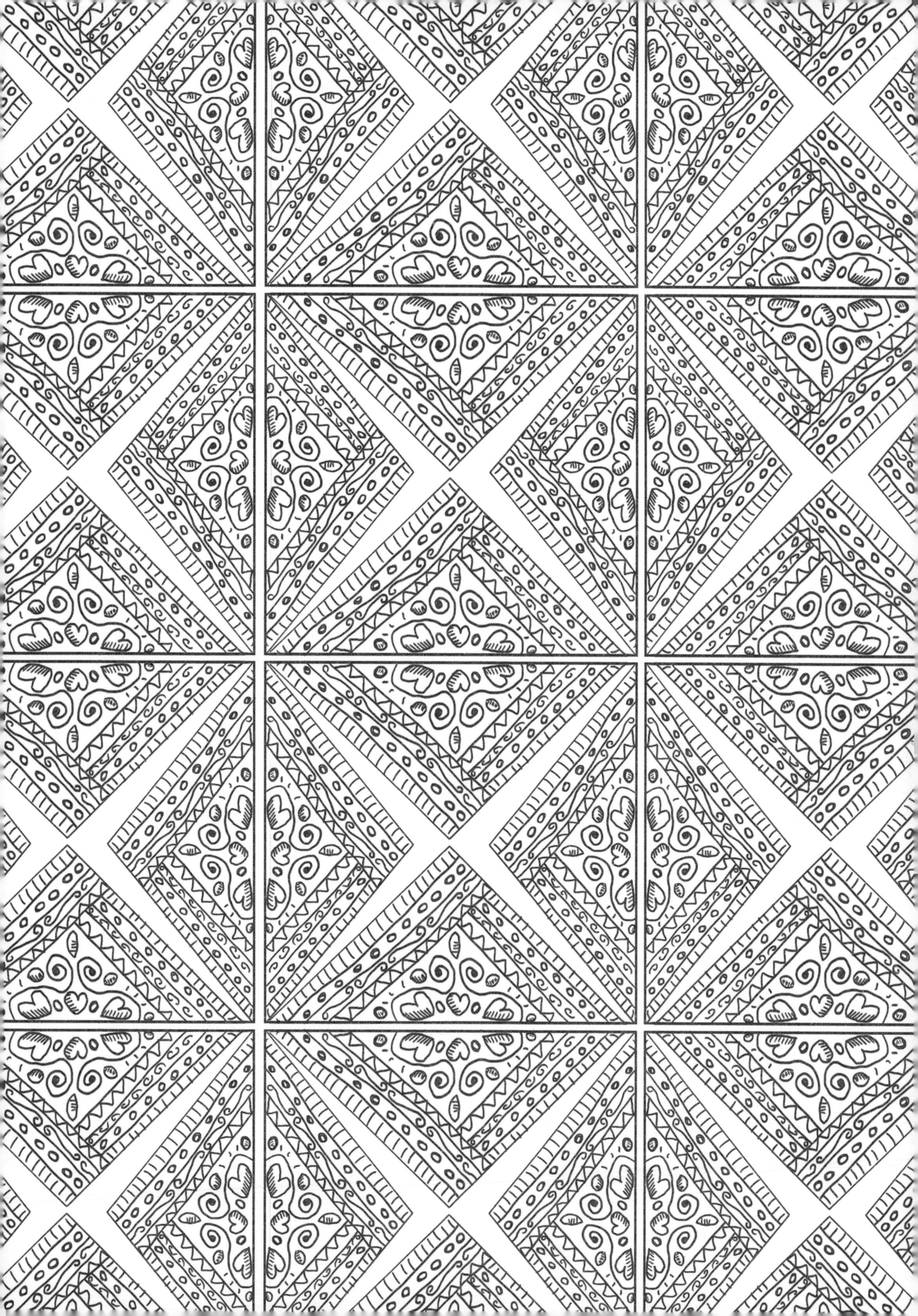

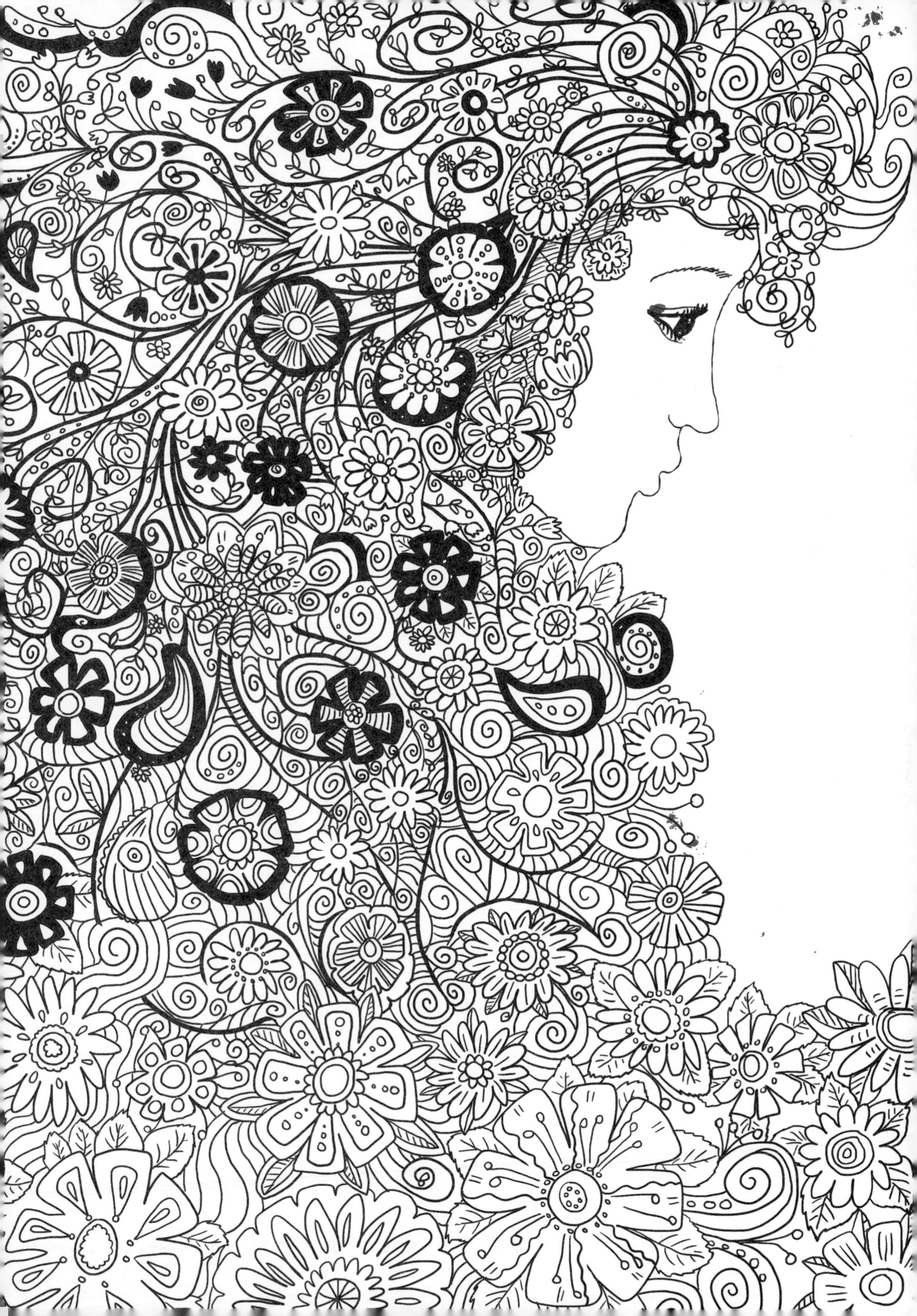

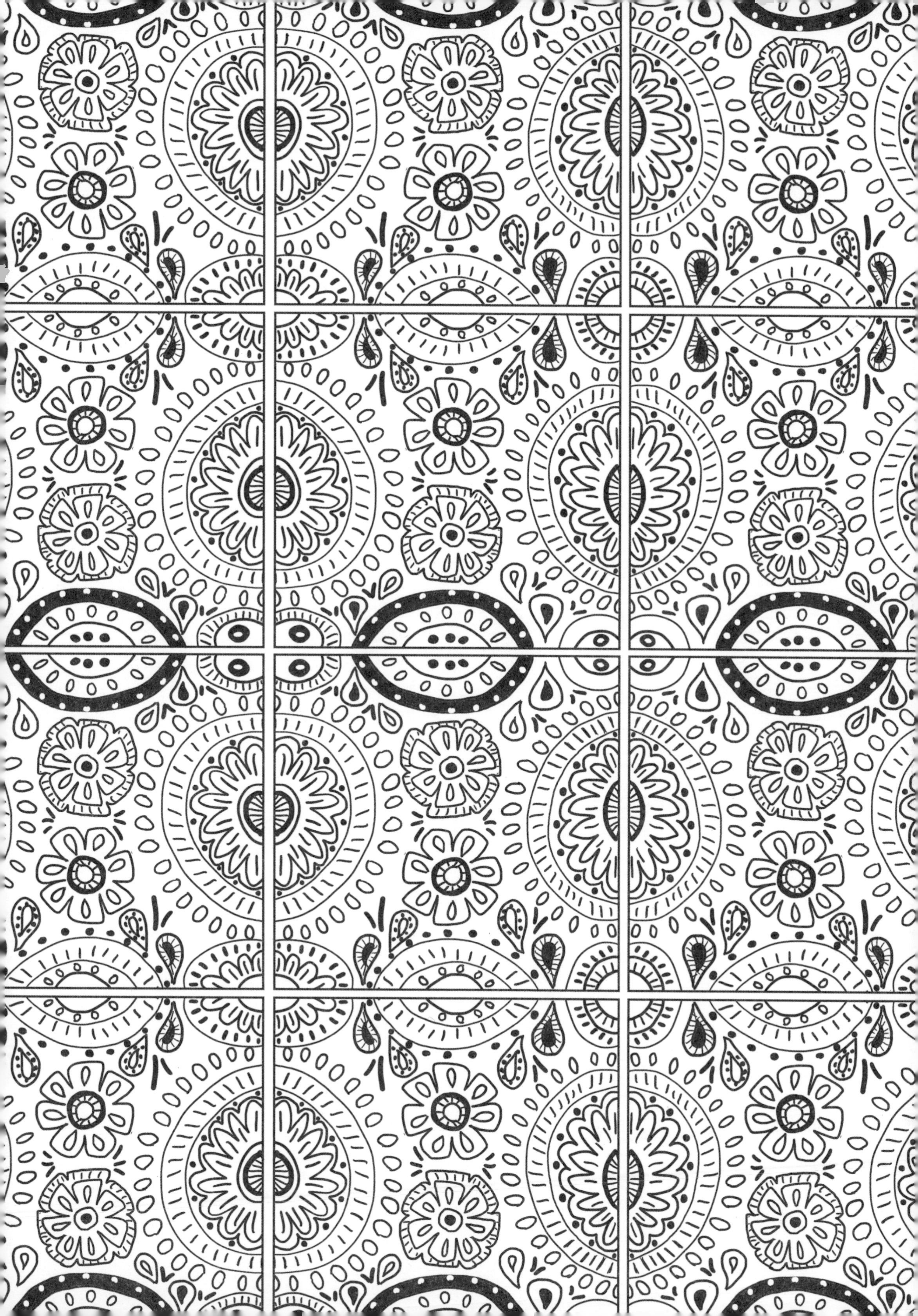

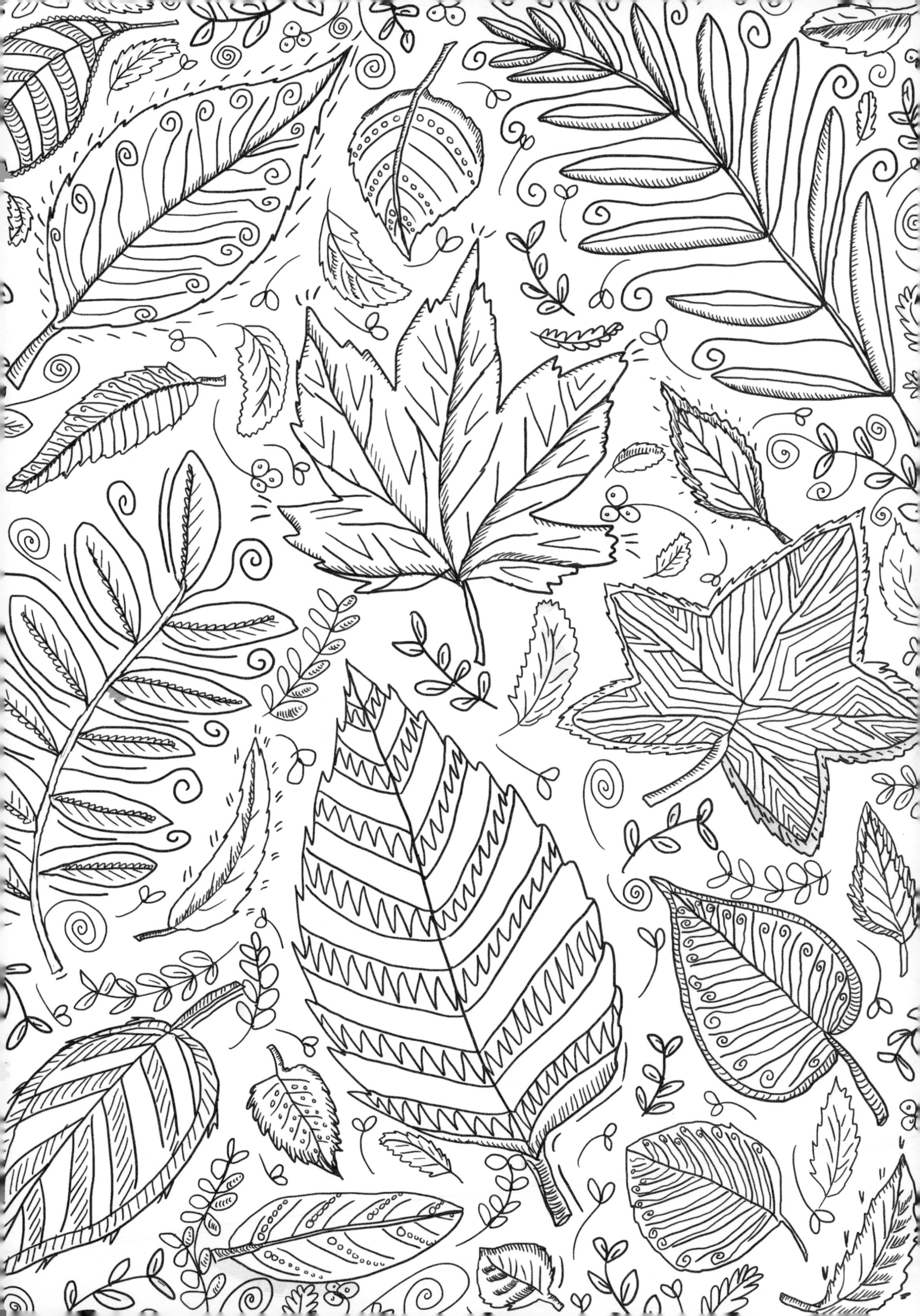

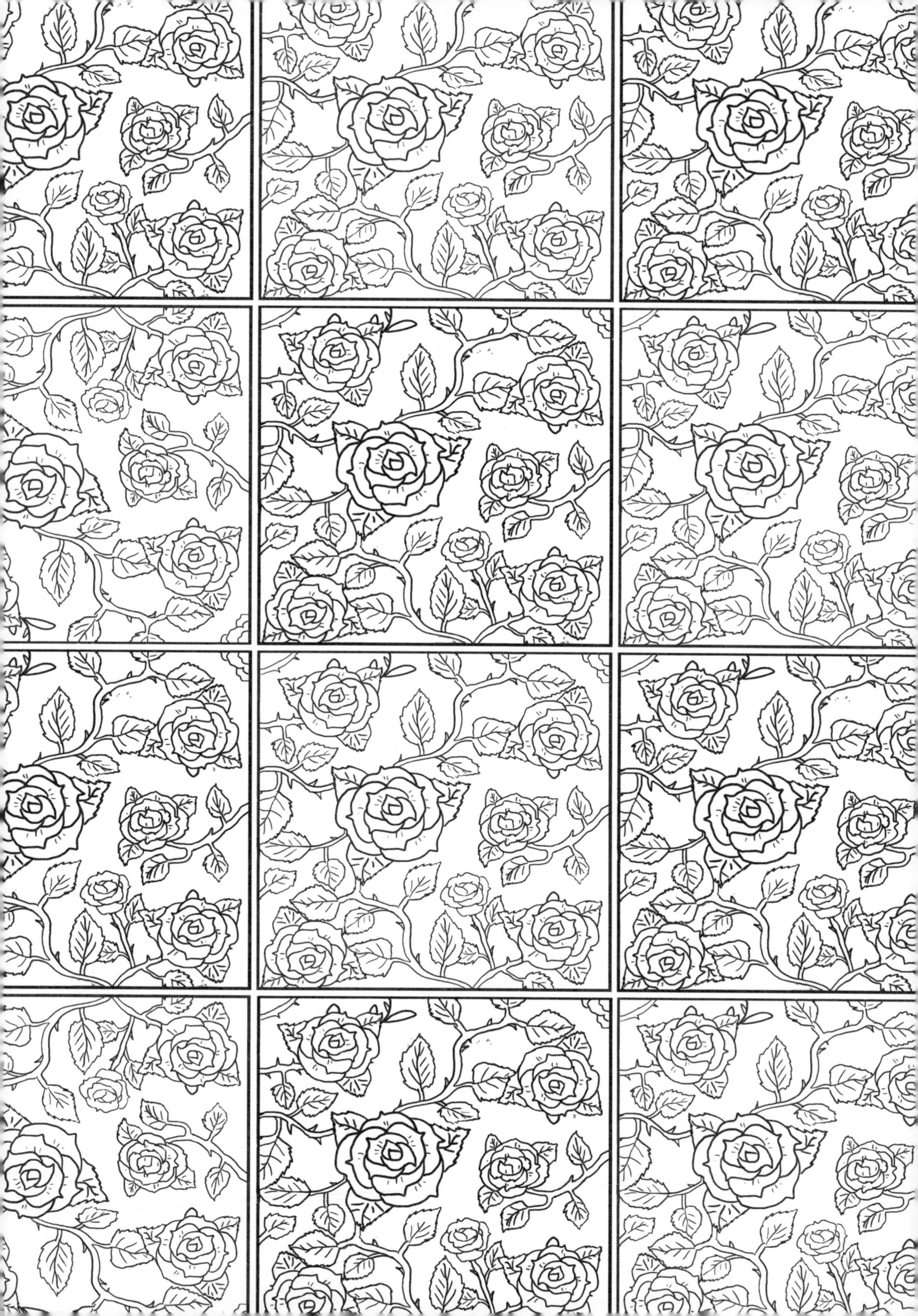

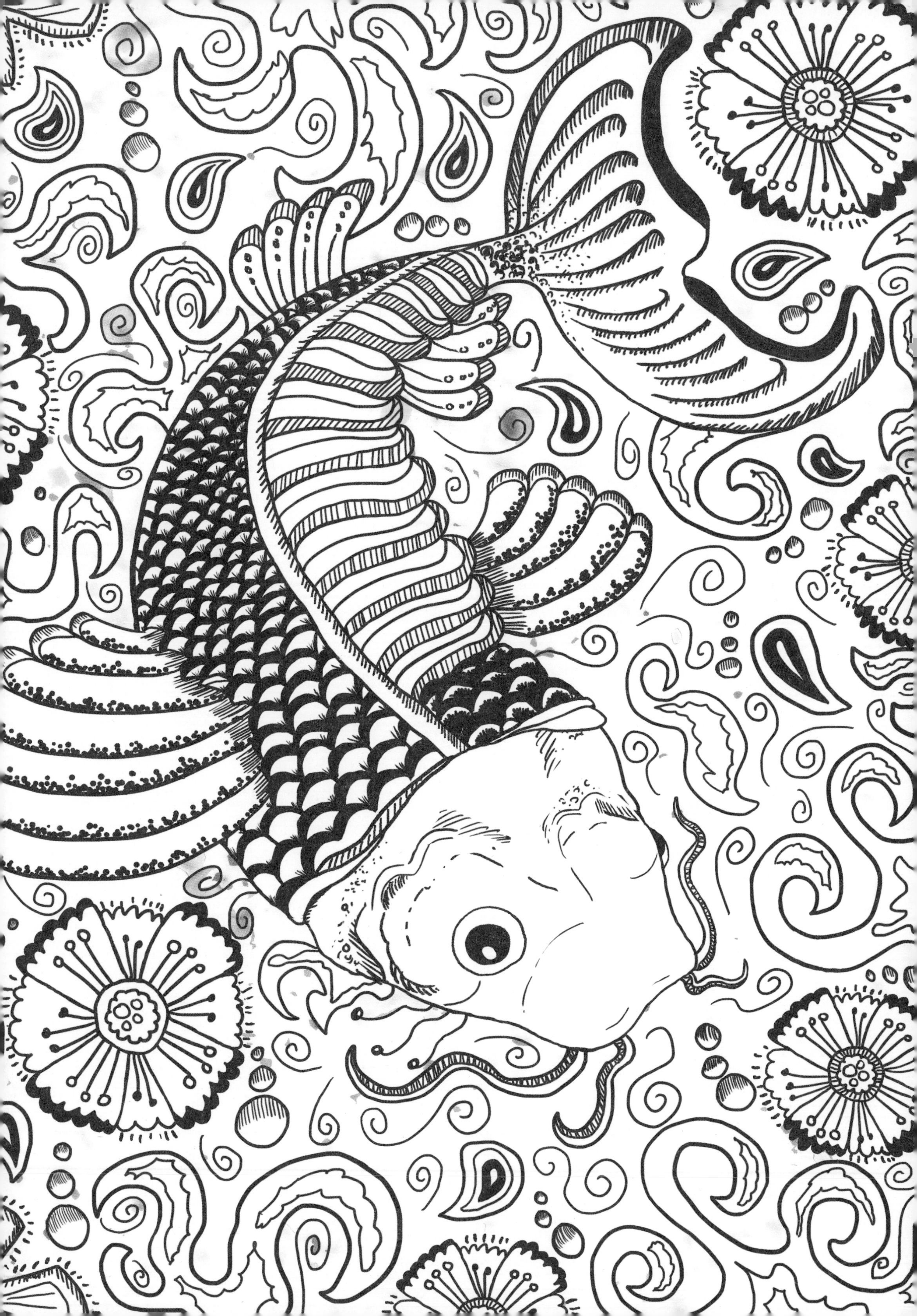

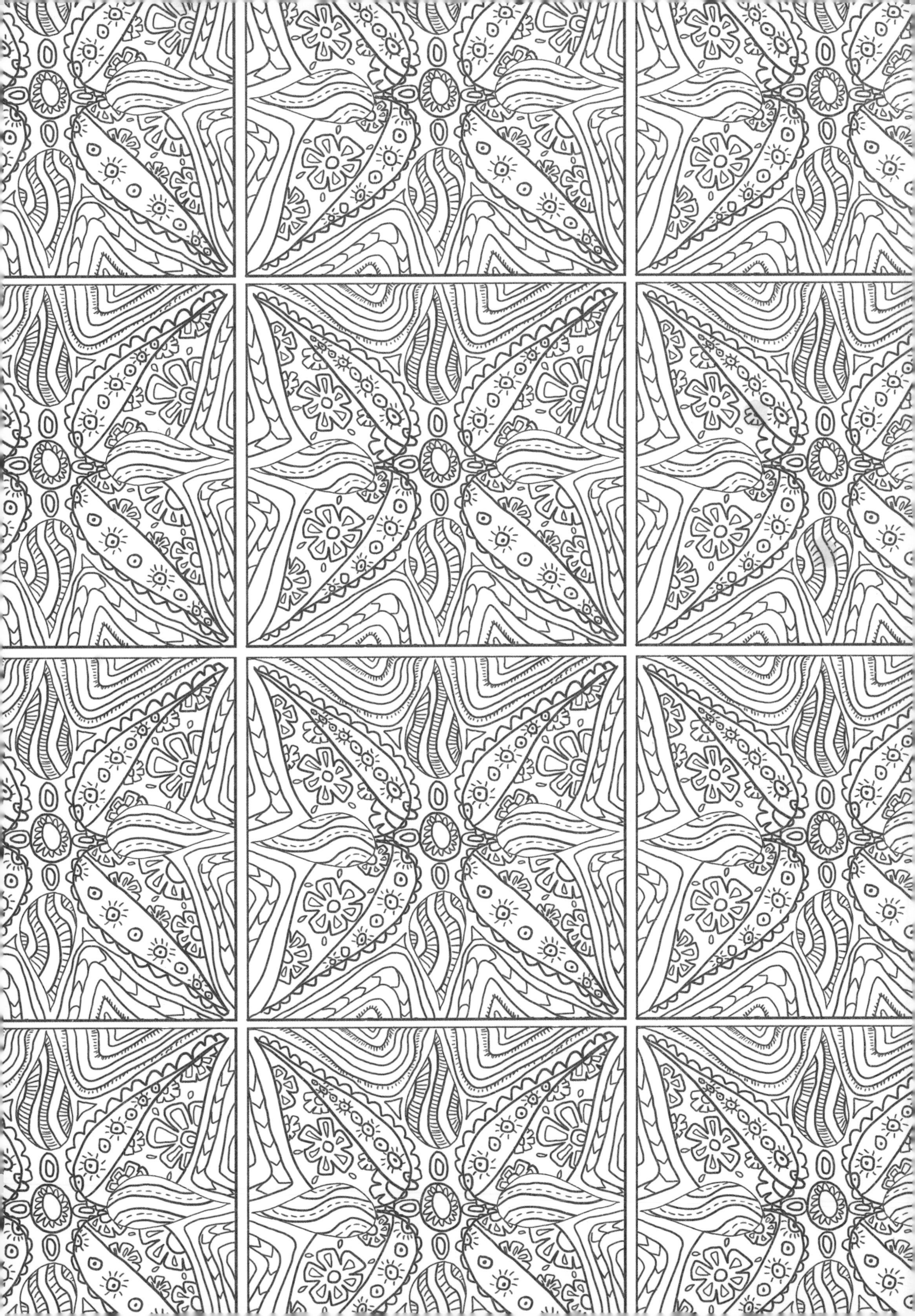

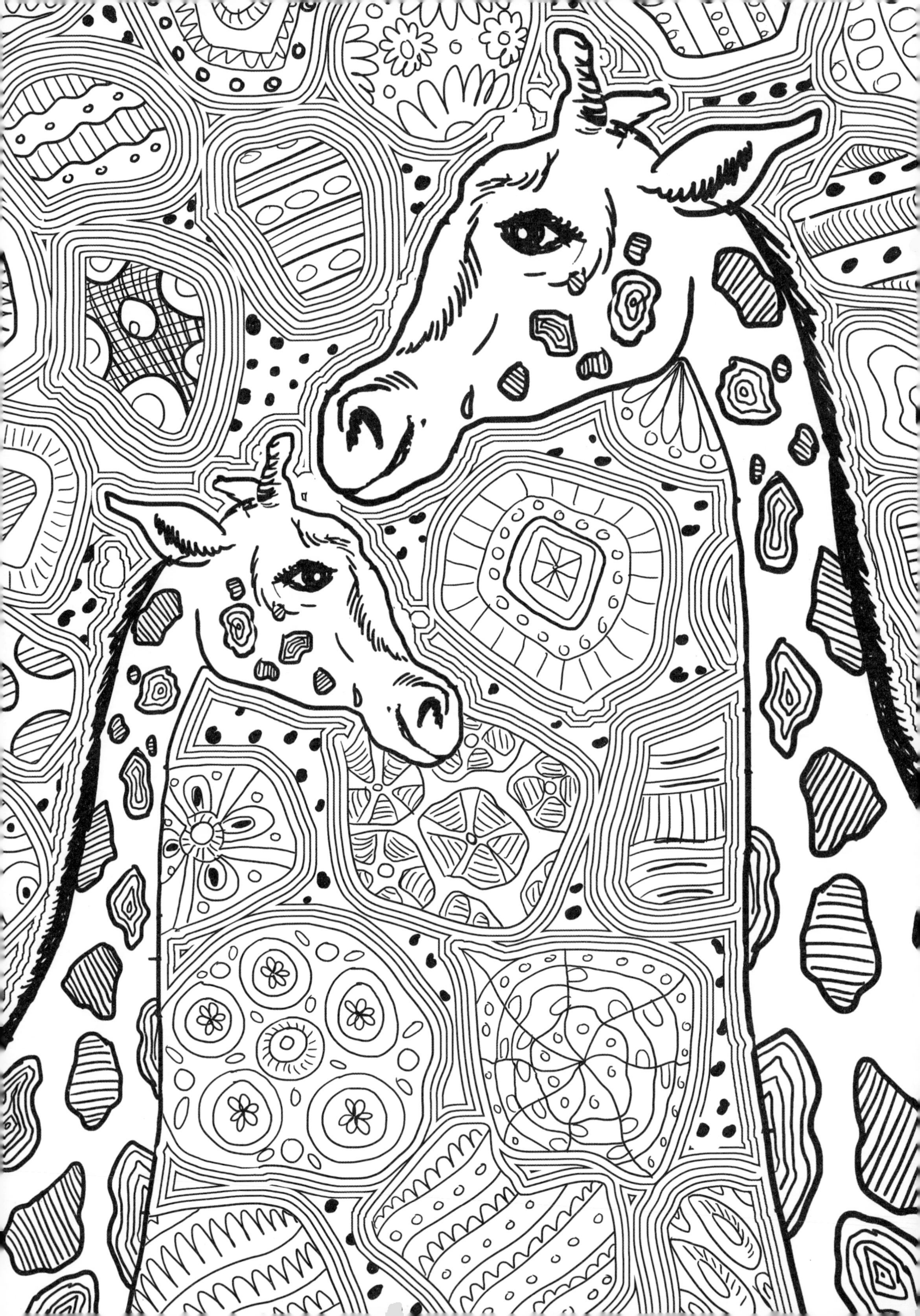

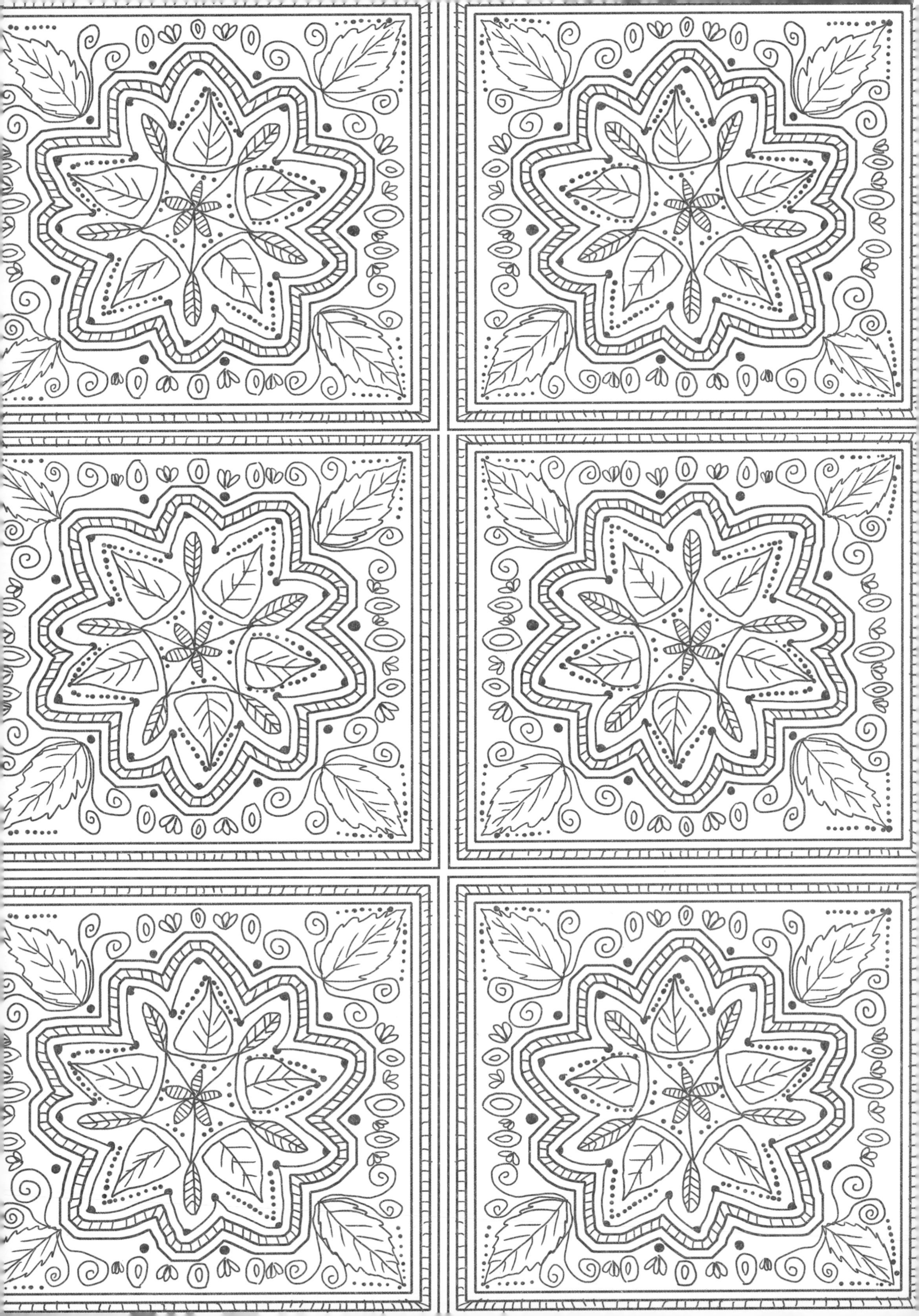

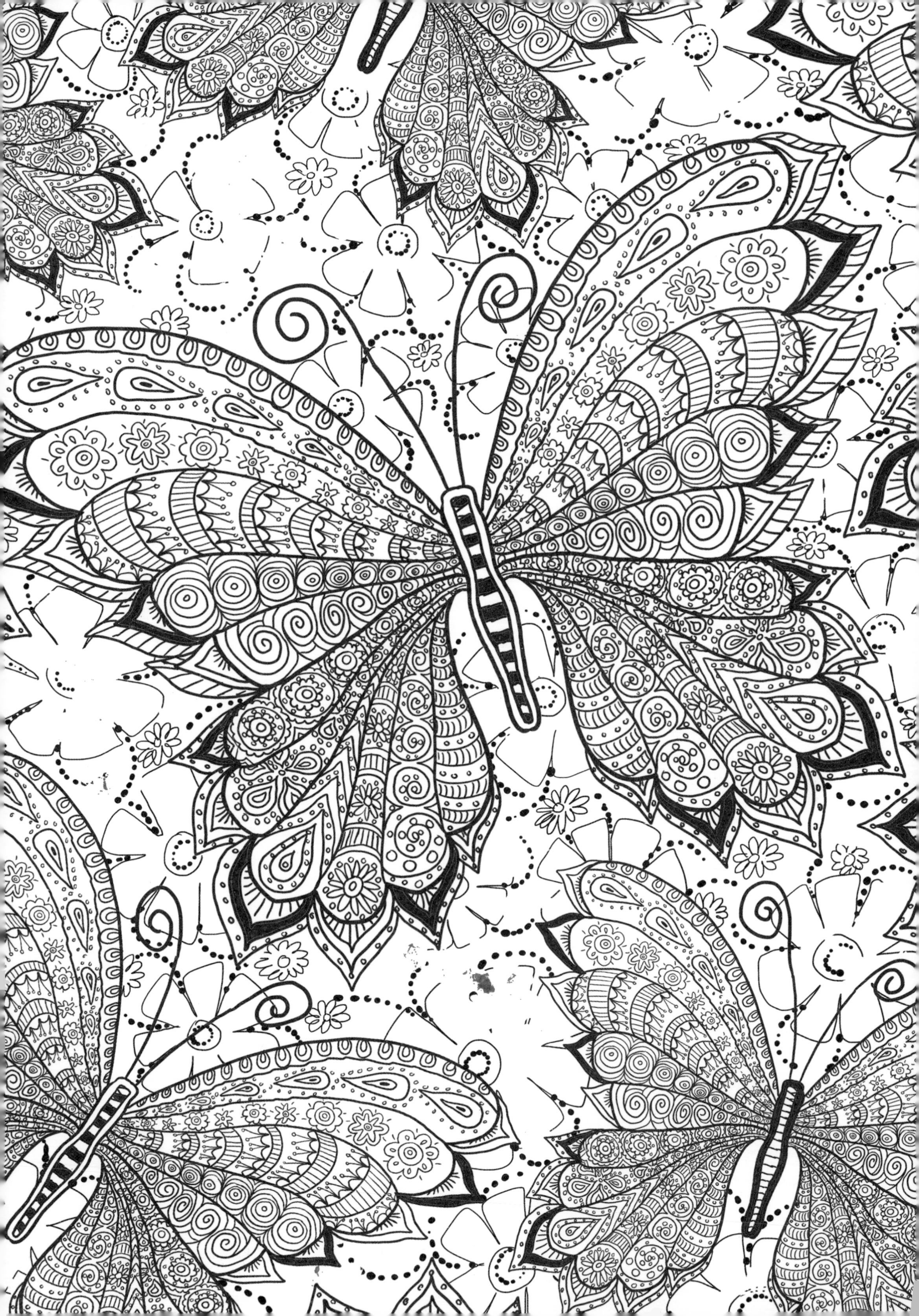

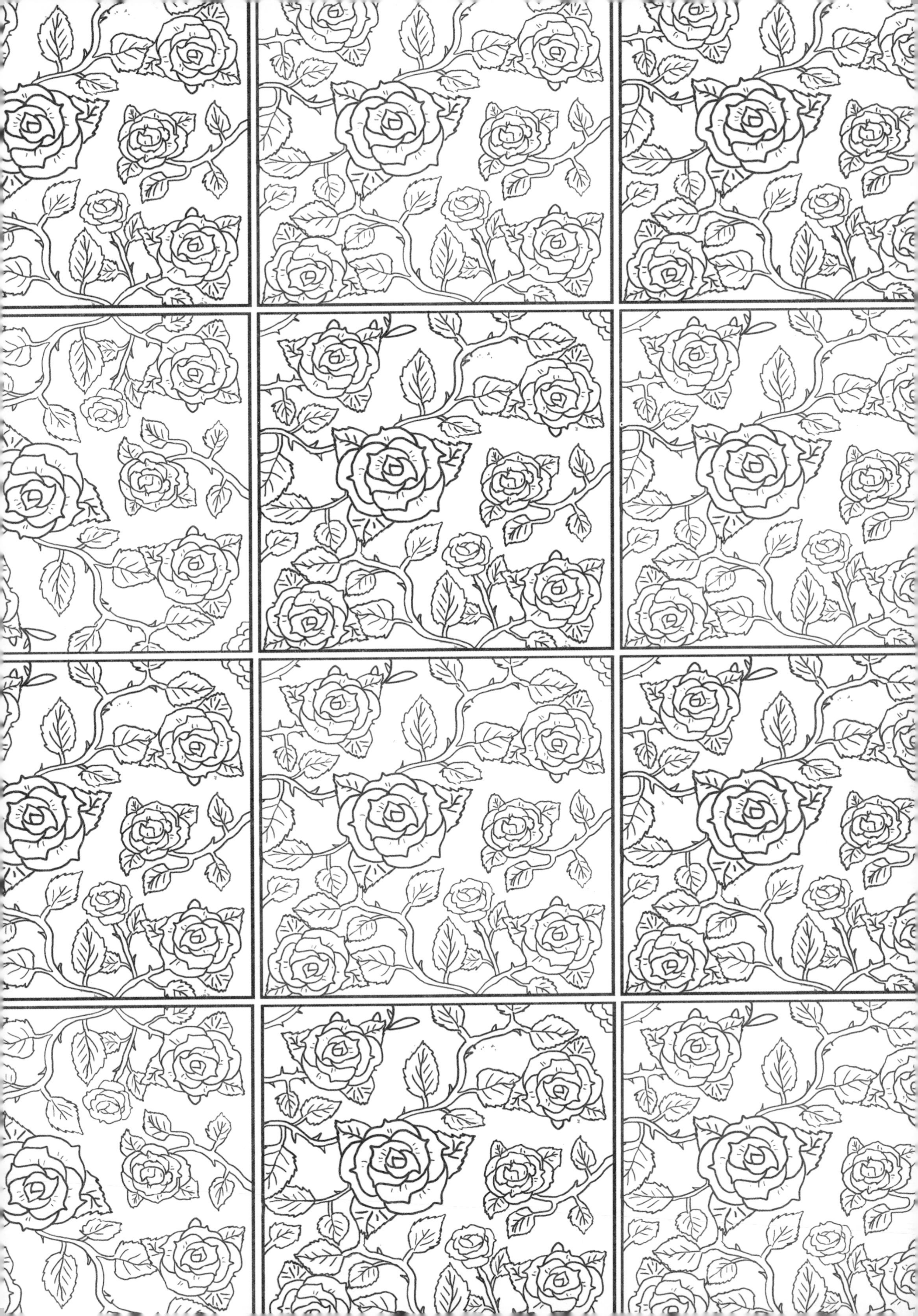

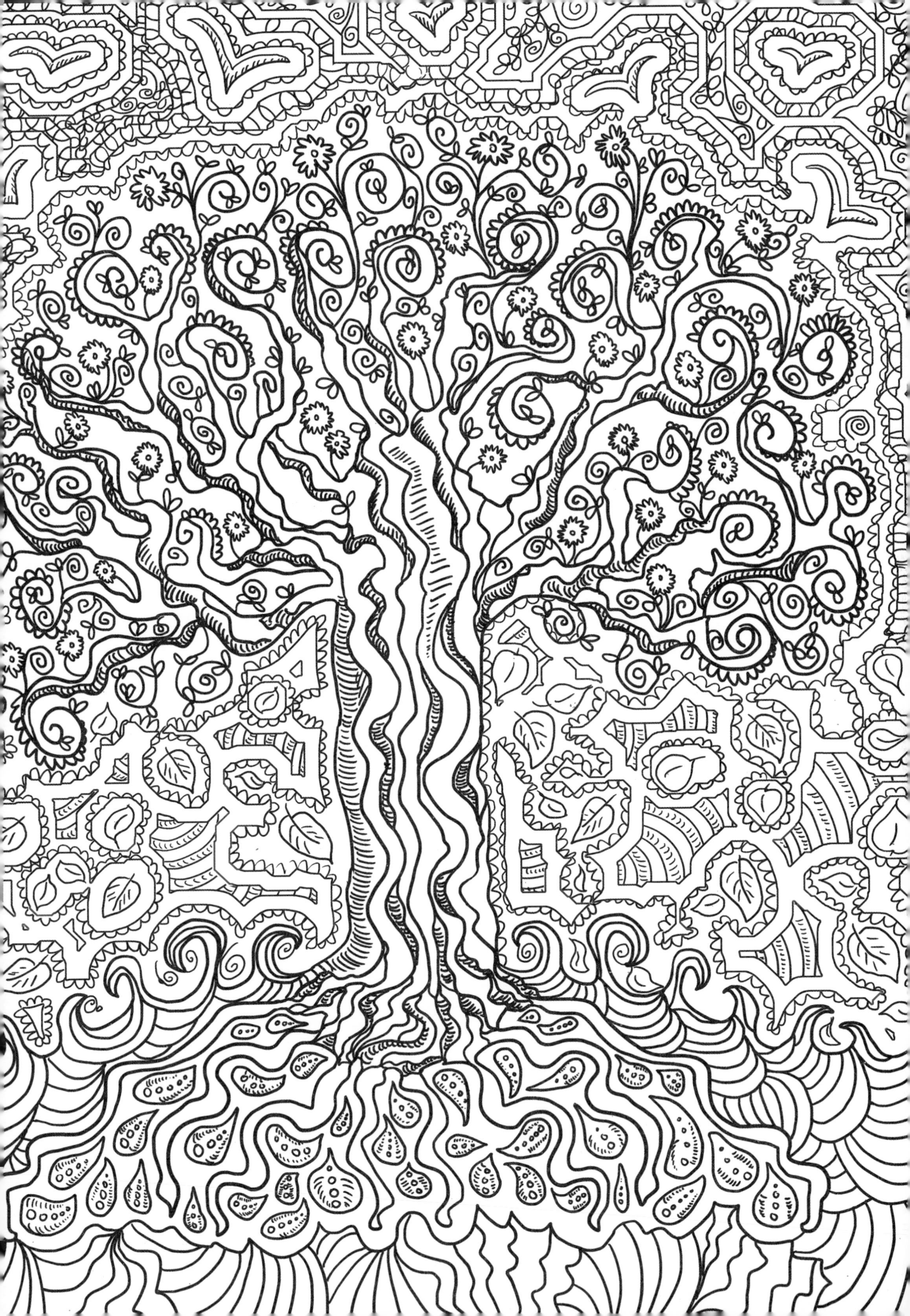

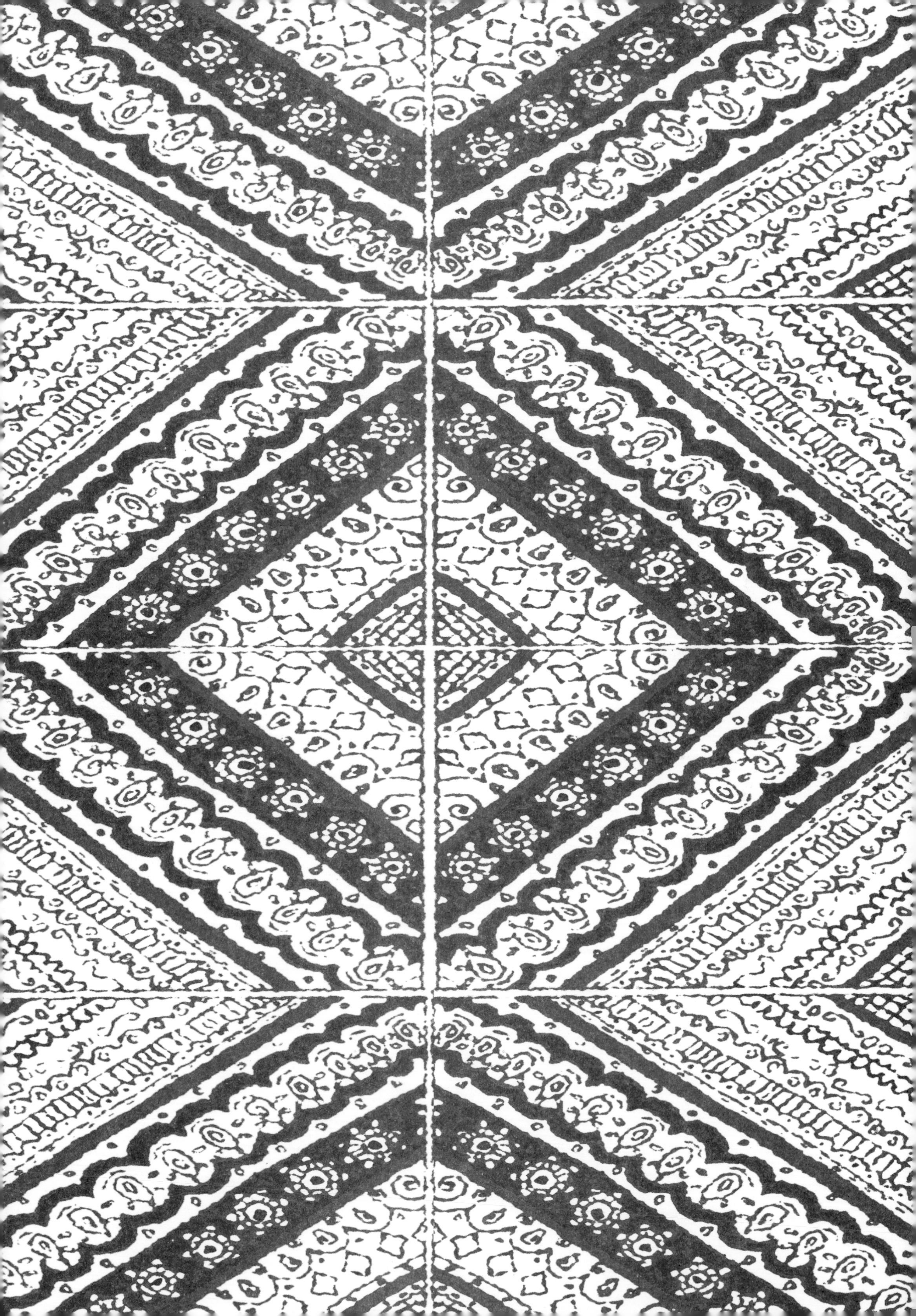

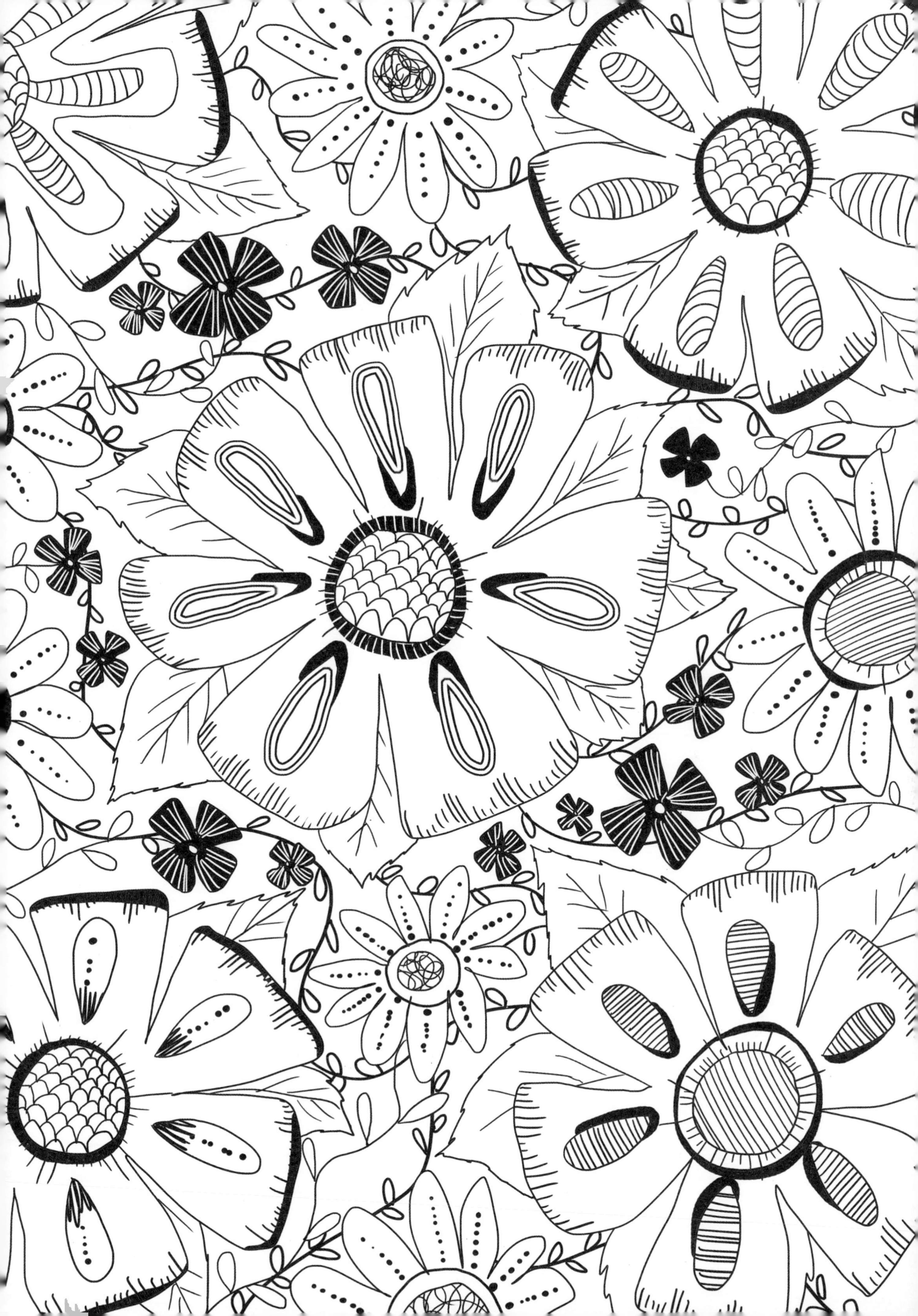

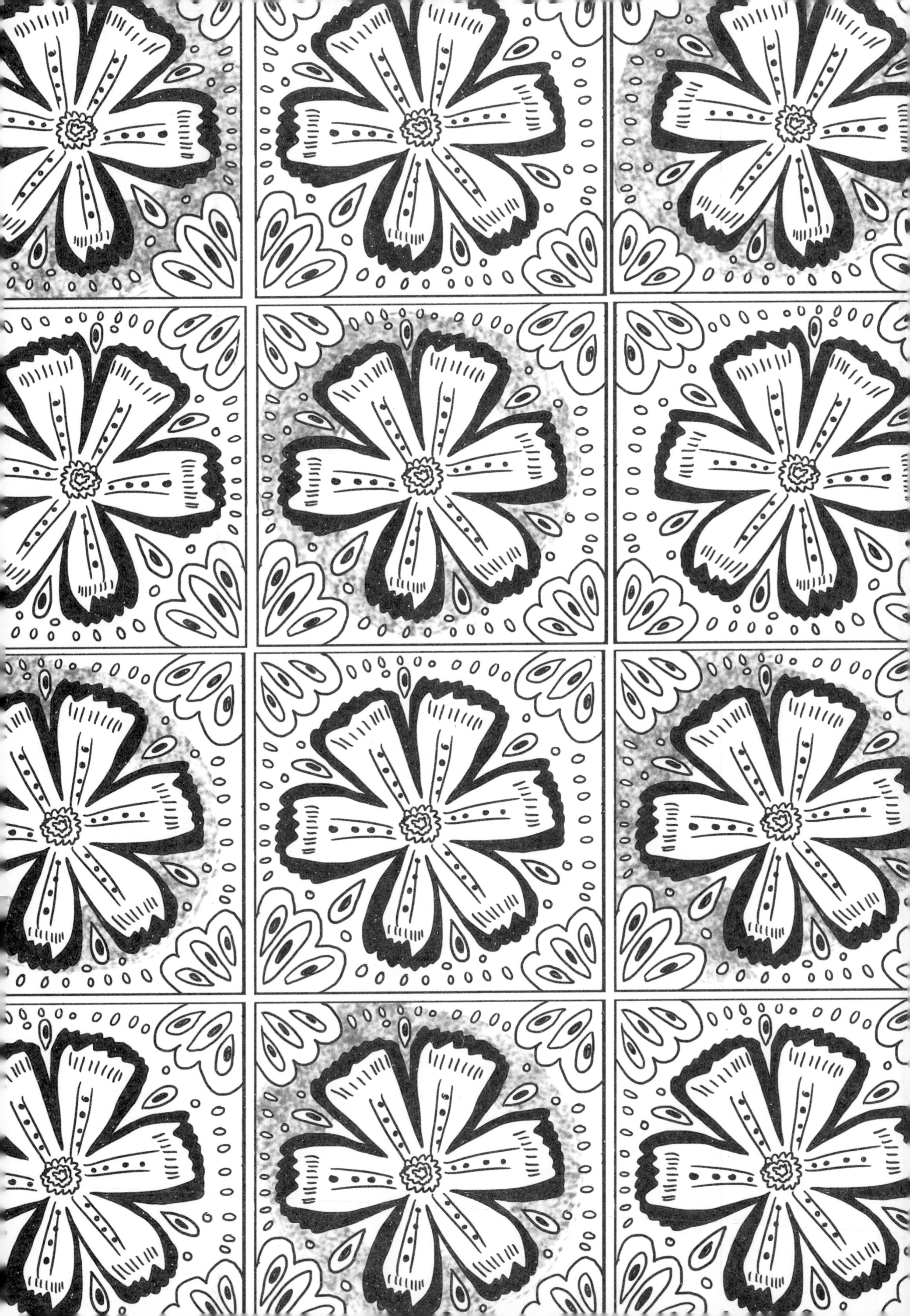

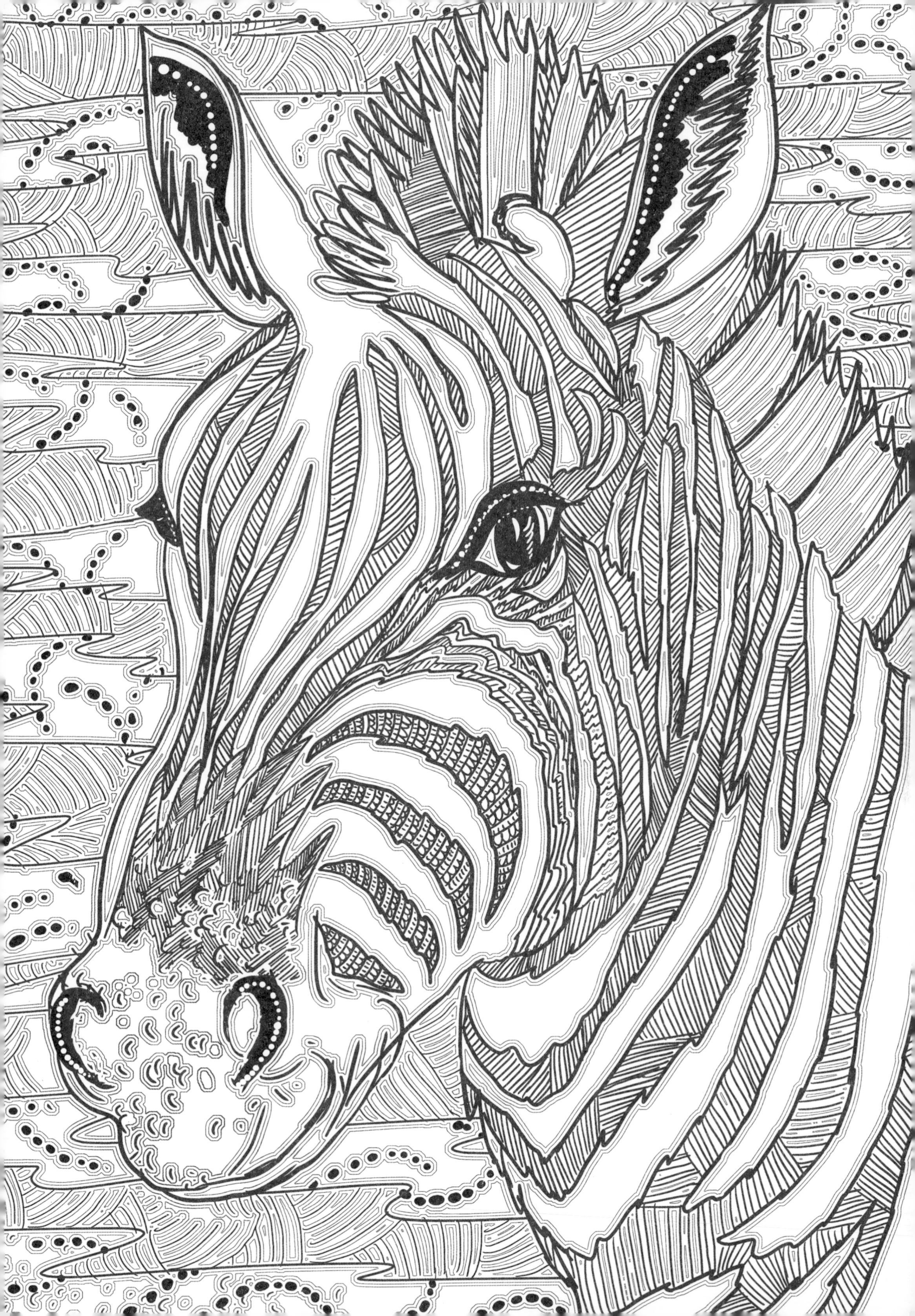

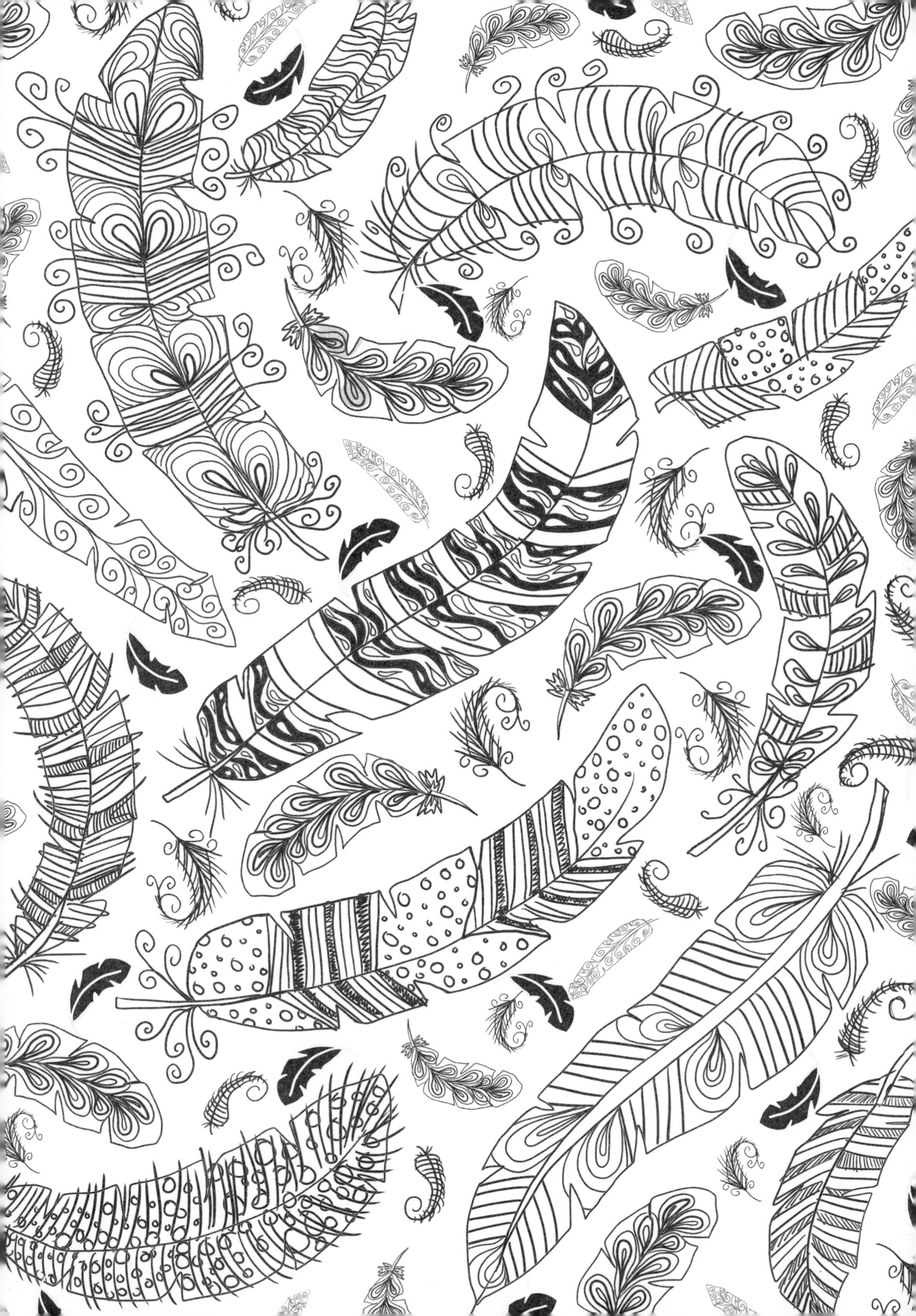

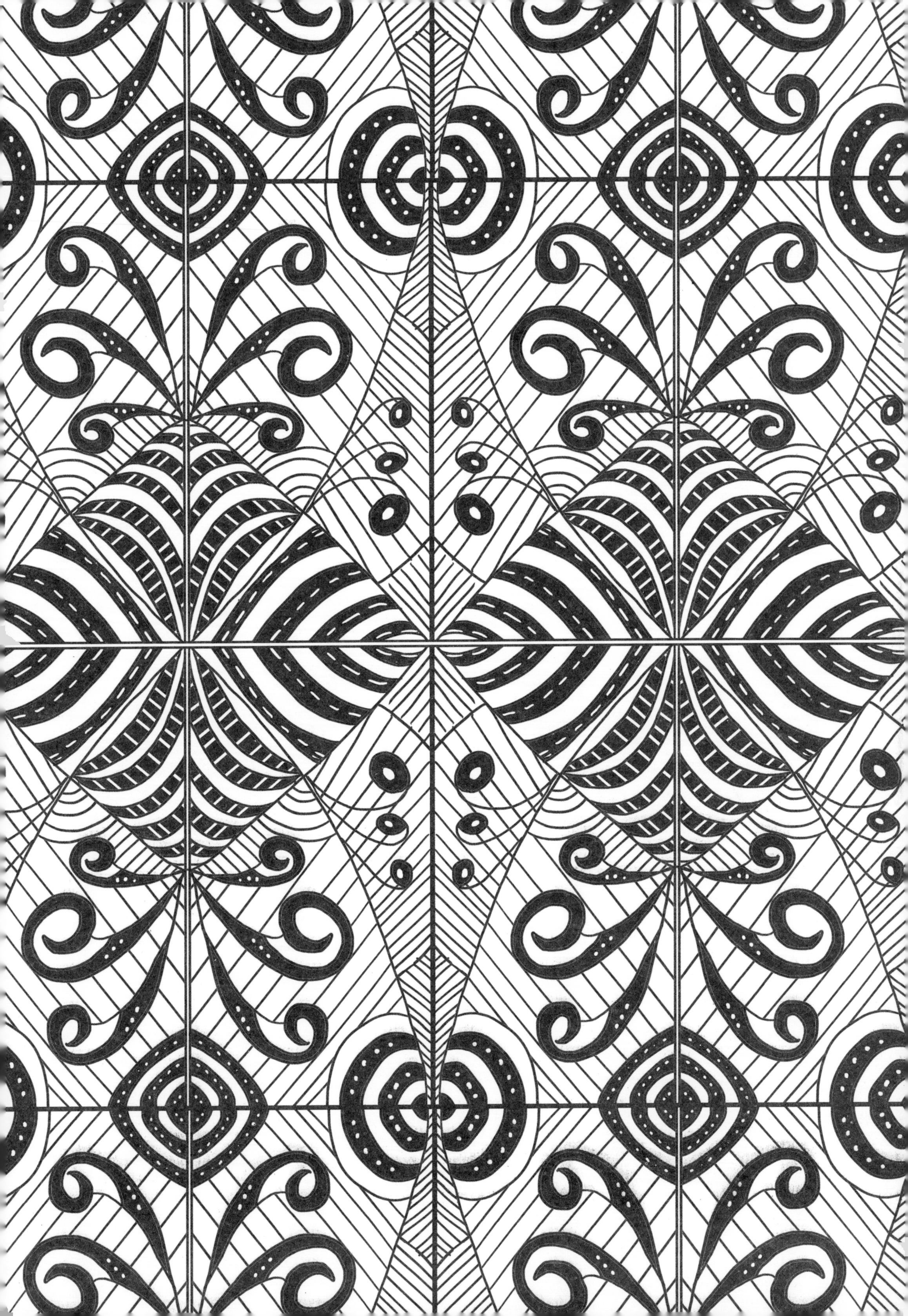

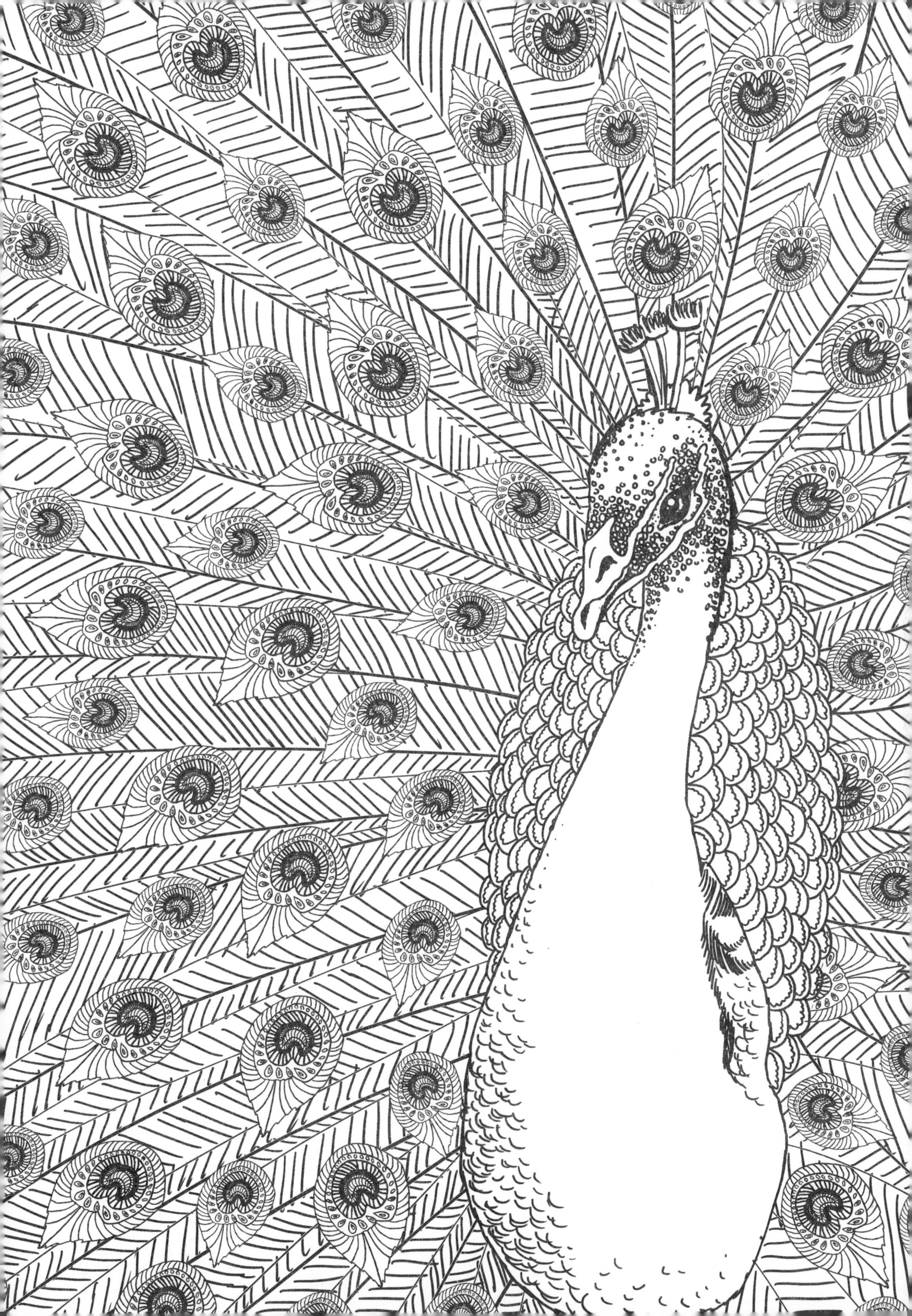

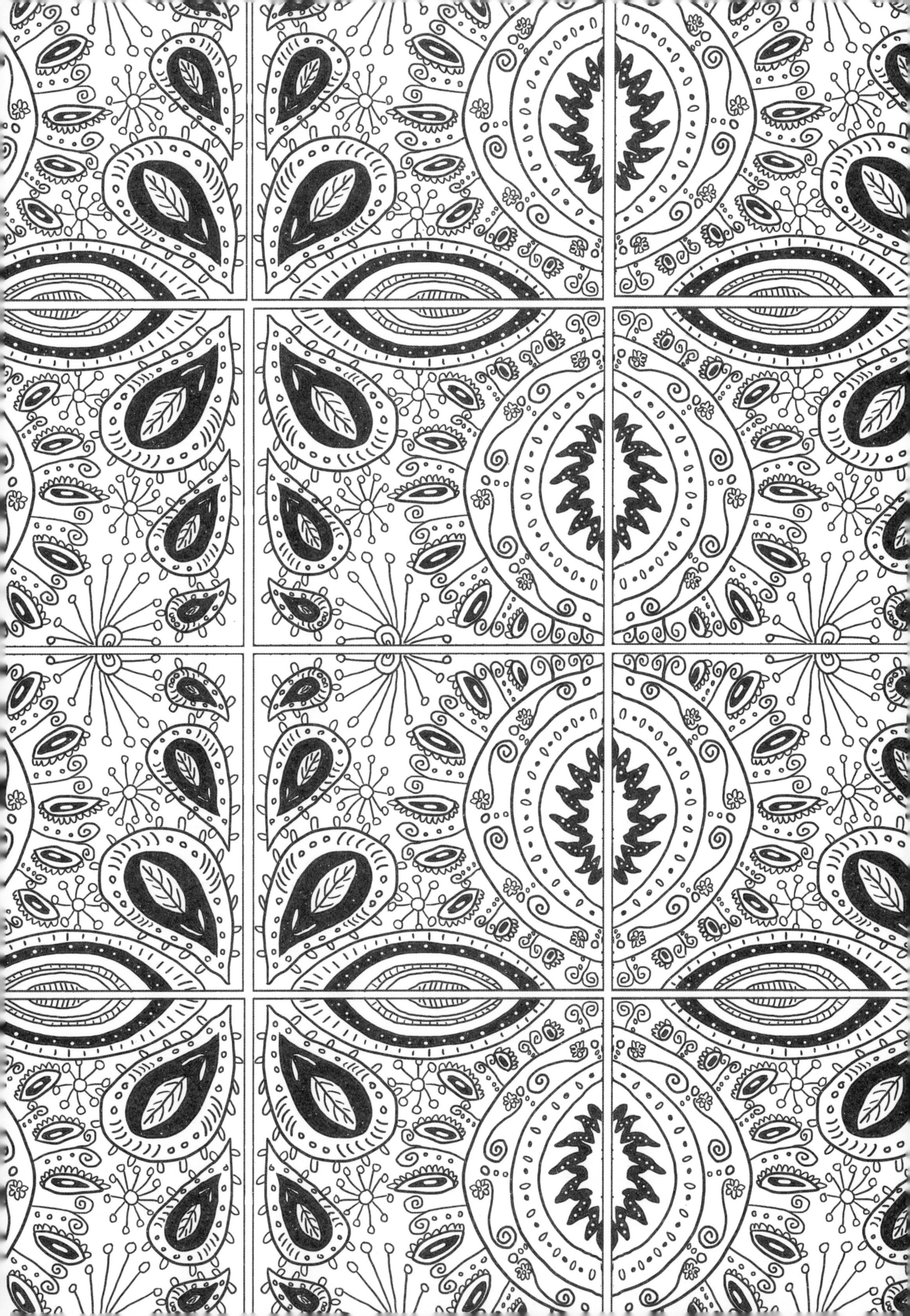

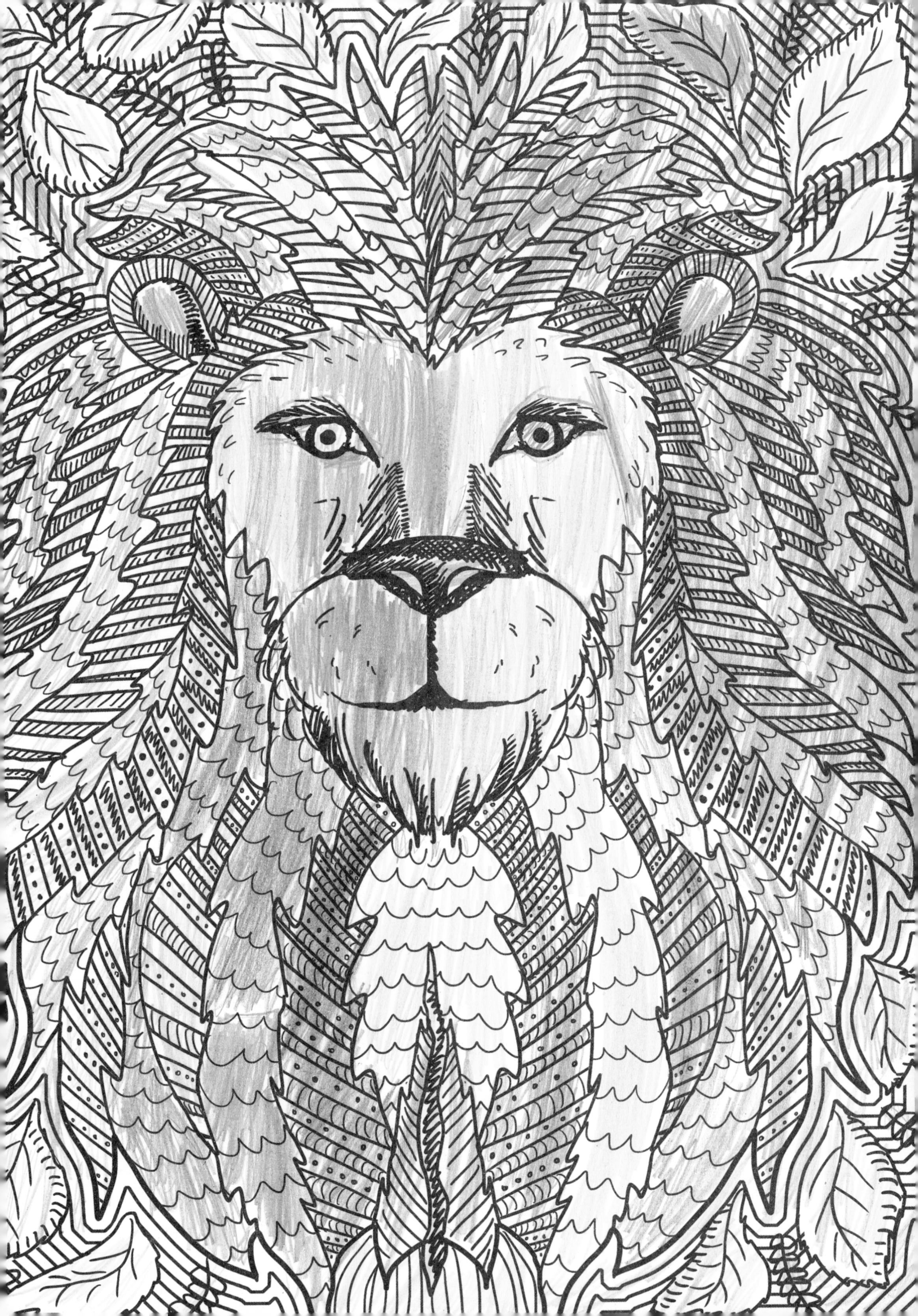

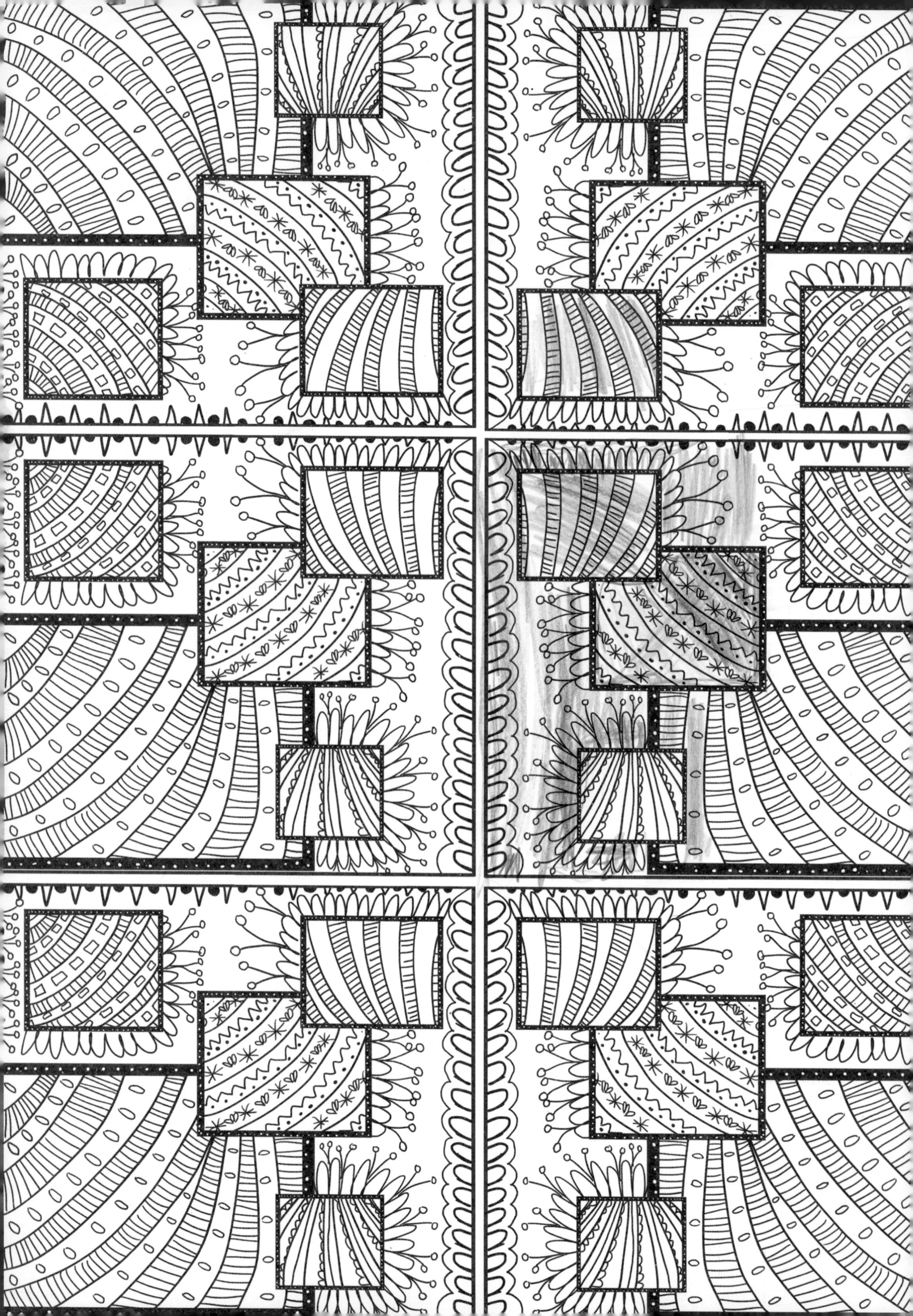